Table of Contents

Part I

Part II

EXPATRIATE TAX QUESTIONNAIRE FOR U.S. CITIZENS LIVING ABROAD

Part III

Part I

Congratulations on deciding to live overseas, now comes the hard part-filing your taxes! I did for over 11 years in Europe and it was some of the most exciting times of my life. I owned a tax office in West Berlin and was also a US Army Reserve Captain taking on the communist threat once a month as a TC Train Commander through the former East Germany and the Soviet checkpoints. When the Soviets called it quits and they "tore down that wall" things changed dramatically in the world. The constant for me however was I had prepared international tax returns for Americans living overseas for several years before the Berlin Wall came down and have been doing them ever since, having several tax offices both in the U.S. and Canada.

This information booklet is broken into two parts: Part 1-general information on all tax aspects of living overseas. Part 2- the general questionnaire that I would need you to fill out and email/fax back to me in order to prepare your return.

Let's get started

The "Foreign earned income exclusion" or <u>FEIE</u>, for Americans living aboard is perhaps the most interesting and challenging part of the U.S. tax code and is constantly changing after Sept,11,2001. The U.S. is perhaps the only modern country (excluding the Philippines) that requires all of it's citizens to file a tax return if they earn money overseas, no matter where they live ,no matter what currency they earn it in (after they have converted their earnings to the official exchange rate).

 NOTE: You can use <u>www.oanda.com/currency</u> for historical currency conversions (typically average exchange rate for the year is used).

Also it is important to note that many tax benefits allowed to U.S. residents are not available to citizens overseas. For example, donations to charities not registered in the U.S. are not tax deductible, property cannot be transferred tax-free to spouses who are <u>not</u> U.S. citizens, Medicare benefits cannot be received to name but a few.

While there have been debates about how much foreign-earned income should be excludable and to whom the provisions should apply. Congress has been very clear, in close to a century since introduction of the modern income tax system, that no law to "tax" based on residency rather than citizenship has ever passed

Congress. As far as we are aware, no such legislation has even been introduced nor voted upon. There have been proposals by academics and interest groups representing Americans living overseas to introduce a "residence-based" tax system similar to almost every other country in the world but it has not received widespread attention and is essentially zero chance of it ever being implemented.

I am not going to discuss the specific income tax rules of the foreign country in which you live or what is referred to as the "host" country in this article, suffice is to say - stay in compliance and do not invade the local taxes for the authorities will have no putting you on the next plane back to the states for breaking their rules. Consultation with your employer ,a good local tax attorney/accountant or the countries taxing authorities is highly recommended.

Yes, you can exclude your earned income, if you live overseas but only if you meet certain requirements (read below) and/or get a tax credit for the foreign taxes paid to the host country but you can't do both on the same income. For the most part it is simplest to exclude your income on IRS form 2555,IRC sec. 911, of the tax code and then get a prorated tax credit for any income above the excluded amounts, presently $95,100 in 2012 ,$92,900 in 2011,$91,500 for 2010 etc, not taking the additional housing exclusion into account which you may qualify for and will be discussed in greater detail later. If you were to use the tax credit in part of in whole you would use IRS form 1116 providing you pay foreign income taxes but again you can't generally take both on the same income source.

Most Americans living abroad fall well below the maximum exclusion amount so filing their return is relatively straight forward. Let's review some basics of the tax code for Americans living overseas and at the end I have included my questionnaire for either this year or past years that you can use so I can prepare your return(s).

FOREIGN EARNED INCOME EXCLUSION

As stated, a U.S. Citizen who lives abroad is taxed on their "worldwide income" which includes both wages, passive income and portfolio income (interest ,dividends ,capital gains ,etc). However, for 2012, a taxpayer may qualify to exclude up to $95,100 of earned income when they file in 2013,they may also be entitled to exclude from income the value of certain meals and lodging provided by their employer but more on that later.

Requirements

All of the following requirements <u>must</u> be met before you are eligible to claim the FEIE (foreign earned income exclusion) on IRS form 2555.

- Your tax home must be in a foreign country.
- You must have foreign earned income, regardless of who pays it, whether it is a foreign based or U.S. based company.
- And there must be at least one of the following:
- A U.S. citizen or a U.S. resident alien was physically present in a foreign country or countries for at least <u>330</u> full days during any period of <u>12 consecutive months</u>, yes that means you may have to delay your fling for you first year abroad until you have lived in your host country for a total of 330 days. This could mean your qualifying days may spread over 2 years requiring you to "prorate" the days for one or both of the years once you have met the 330 days of residency in the foreign country.

Calculating your days overseas-some time line examples:

1. <u>Simple example</u>- you arrive in the foreign country on Jan.1, 2012-you live in the country for 330 days continuously. You qualify to file for the FEIE on Dec. 1,2012.

2. <u>A little more complicated example</u>- you arrive in the foreign country on July1,2012 and live in the country continuously for 330 days. You qualify to file for the FEIE on Jun 1, 2013. You should file an extension (form 4868) on April 15th ,2013 which will extend your filing deadline till Oct.15,2013. If you owe any more than you need to pay them with your extension on April 15th.

3. <u>Complicated example</u>- Your first year you arrive in country on Jan.1, 2012   you live in the country for 180 days (Till July 1,2013) but then go home for over 30 days (July 2 – August 3,2012). Your clock resets to August 4 for the 330 days in country and you don't qualify for the FEIE till August 4,2013.

Once you have qualified as a "bona fide" residence however the stick 30 day reset of the clock rule does not go into effect as long as you intend to stay in the foreign country, you have not submitted a statement to the authorities that you plan to leave the country and you continue to pay your foreign income taxes.

Note: There is a waiver of the time requirements for taxpayers who must leave a foreign country because of war, civil unrest, or similar adverse conditions. Each year, the IRS releases a list of countries that qualify for this exemption.

Tax Home

Determining the tax home uses the following progression from 1 to 4:

1. The *regular place of business* or post of duty, regardless of where you maintain the family home.
2. The *main place of business* if the taxpayer has two or more places of business.
3. The *place the taxpayer regularly lives* if there is no place of business.
4. *No place* if the tax player has no place of business and no place of regular residence.

A taxpayer who does not meet one of the first three situations listed above has no tax home and is considered an "itinerant" worker. An itinerant worker is never away from home and therefore has no travel expenses (though they may have transportation expenses such as airfare or a ship or bus ticket).
When a taxpayer leaves the U.S. and works away from their principal place of business ,home or employment, the following travel expenses are deductible:

1. Transportation costs to and from the place(s) outside the "tax home".
2. Living expenses while away from the tax home overnight such as room and board.

However before considering your travel expenses away from home, you have to establish your "tax home" for it may generate a deduction if you work at more than one work site during the day.

Main Place of Business

A person's tax home is the entire city or general area where the principal place of business, employment, or post of duty is located, regardless of where the taxpayer's family residence is located. If a taxpayer has more than one place of business or employment, the tax home is the <u>main</u> place of business determined with these three factors in mind:

1. The amount of income earned in each area.
2. The total time ordinarily spent in performing duties in each area.
3. The level of business activity in each area.

Foreign Country

This term includes any territory under a sovereignty of a government other than the U.S. It does not include Antarctica or U.S. possessions. It does include the country's airspace and territorial waters, but not international waters to the airspace above them.

Foreign Earned Income Defined

This is income received for services performed during a period in which you meet both of the following requirements:

1. Their tax home is in a foreign country.
2. They meet either the "bona fide" residence test or the "physical presence" test- read below.

Foreign earned income also includes the FMV (fair market value) of employer provided property or facilities such as lodging, meals, or use of a car. It also includes allowances or reimbursements for such items as:

- Cost - of - living allowances.
- Overseas differential.
- Family allowance.
- Employer gross - up to account for such items as foreign taxes owed by employee or income tax equalization.
- Reimbursement for education or educational allowance.
- Home leave allowance.
- Quarters allowance.
- Reimbursement for moving or moving allowance (unless excludable).

Foreign earned income <u>does not</u> include:

- The value of meals and lodging excluded because the meals and lodging were furnished for the employer's convenience.
- Pension or annuity payments including Social Security benefits.
- Pay received as an employee of the U.S. government.
- Amounts included because of employers' contributions to a nonexistent employee trust or to a nonqualified annuity contract.
- Any unallowable moving expense deduction that is that recaptured.
- Payments received after the end of the tax year following the tax year in which services that earned income were performed.

Source of Earned Income

The source of your earned income is the place where the services are performed, when <u>or how the payments are made as no affect on the source of the income.</u>

There are special rules that apply to determine foreign earned income and unearned income from the sole proprietorship or from a partnership or what is called self employment. See IRS publications 54, the tax guide for U.S. citizens and resident aliens abroad, to pursue this topic and to study other topics in greater depth.

The "Bona Fide Residents Test" Vs. "Physical Presence Test"

When claiming the FEIE, a taxpayer may exclude income under either test (provided they meet all of the requirements)and must make this election on an annual basis.

Both tests require a tax home to be in a foreign country. The "Bona fide" residence test appeals to a taxpayer who has some evidence to prove that they plan to make a permanent home in that foreign country i.e. paid foreign income taxes ,bought a home in the foreign country ,married a native of the country ,have a driver's license in that country, and have not submitted a statement to the host county that that do not plan to leave anytime soon ,even though they may not have lived 330 full days outside the U.S. in that country.

Note: A full day, for the purpose of determining the physical presence tests, is a period of 24 consecutive hours, beginning at midnight.

Electing The Exclusion

The FEIE is an ongoing choice and you need to stay current but once made, you **cannot**:

- Take a Foreign Tax Credit or deduction for taxes on income that can be excluded ,IRS form 1116,unless you have income over the excludable amount.
- Claim Earned Income Credit (EIC).
- Open a traditional Roth IRA based on excluded earned income.
- Claim the additional Child Tax Credit based on excluded earned income.
- Use the tax rate schedule based on taxable income. Instead, a US taxpayer must figure the tax using the tax rates that would have applied had they not claimed the exclusions.

The initial choice is made by filing Form 2555, *Foreign Earned Income*, generally, as part of a return:

- Filed by the due date (including extensions).
- Amending a timely - filed return.
- Filed within one year from the original due date of the return (determined without regard to any exceptions).

See IRS publication 54 for special cases in which returns may be filed outside these timeframes and a US citizen may be given a onetime amnesty for failing to file his or her back return(s) while living overseas. Generally, in order to qualify for these special circumstances, you must have lived and worked abroad and have never filed forms 2555 in the past, this could go back indefinitely as long as the IRS has not discovered this fact. If you are going to use this "loophole" write on top the top of form 1040, "filed pursuant to section 1.911 " The choice remains in effect until revoked by the IRS for they may still disallow it. Of course any late filing fees and penalties may still be applied. As always, stay in compliance with both the IRS and your host country's tax rules for the IRS is now setting up offices at major airports to catch US citizens who have not filed in several years and have basically dropped off the tax rolls.

Foreign Tax Credit-Form 1116

Most taxpayers take this credit if they have a brokerage account invested in foreign securities and foreign taxes were withheld in their account. Based on the foreign tax treaty, the US financial institution (Fidelity , Schwab etc.) must withhold- usually around 15% and pay that back to the foreign country (again this varies from country to country). To take this dollar for dollar credit you must file form 1116- on your tax return and your (passive) income must:

1. Have all foreign sourced income taxes withheld is reported from either interest (1099int),dividends (1099Div) of form K-1.
2. All dividend income received was from shares of stock held more than 15 days.
3. Form 4563 is not being filed or income is not from sources within Puerto Rico
4. All foreign taxes are legally owed and not eligible for refund.
5. All foreign taxes are paid to countries that are recognized by the U.S. and they do not support terrorism.

As stated earlier if you are paying income taxes to the host country you can take an income tax credit (form 1116) but you can't take a credit and exclude your income (form 2555) on the same income. If you earn a lot of money overseas it is simplest to exclude your income first on IRS form 2555,IRC sec. 911, of the tax code and then get a prorated tax credit for any income above the excluded amounts, presently $95,100 in 2012 ,$92,900 in 2011,$91,500 for 2010 etc,.

If you do elect to take the foreign taxes paid as a credit only here are a few things to keep in mind. First of all income on the 1116,part 1 is divided into 5 types of income:

1. Passive income- portfolio income such as interest, dividends,K-1 (read above) etc..
2. General Income-earned wages.
3. Section 901 (j) income- taxes paid to or accrued by certain countries that do not qualify for the foreign tax credit.
4. Income resourced by treaty- if the tax treaty has been renegotiated between the US and that original income has been "resourced".
5. Lump sum distribution- lump-sum distribution from certain types of pension plans.

Make sure if you take the tax credit that you categorize your income into the right groups listed above. Again wages earned overseas will fall into group 2:"general income".

When you convert your income taxes make sure you have the right conversion rate (part 2, 1116) use **www.oanda.com/currency** for the conversion rate for any given year. Make sure you are only converting income taxes and not sales tax, real estate taxes, use tax etc.

Carry forward of your foreign taxes paid:

The exception to taking the FEIE (form 2555) vs. the tax credit(form 1116) is if you plan to work in a country or countries that have higher tax rates than the U.S. It would likely benefit you to make the election to get the tax credit. In fact, making the election might be advantageous because you might be restricted from using it in the future and lose any credit for the income tax paid in any given year. However a taxpayer who may not be able to use the full amount of qualified foreign taxes paid would be allowed a one year carry back and a 10 year carryover of the unused foreign taxes paid, part 3,1116. Make sure you make note of it on your tax return for this is often overlooked by the tax preparer from one year to year to the next.

Reporting your Financial Interests In Foreign Countries

U.S. taxpayers living abroad and at home who have foreign bank accounts, foreign stock accounts, and other financial accounts must disclose that information in Question 7, Part III, Schedule B of the Form 1040.

Form TDF 90-22.1 (Treasury form not a IRS form) is required to be filed by U.S. citizens and permanent residents who have financial interest in or signature or other authority over any financial accounts, including bank, securities, or other types of financial accounts in a foreign country, if the aggregate (total) value of these financial accounts exceeded $10,000 at any time during the tax year (*the highest value of each account during the tax year combined with all other foreign accounts exceeds $10,000 at any one time during the year*). This form is be filed separately from your regular tax return and should not be attached to your 1040. The form must be received by the Detroit US Treasury Address on June 30th of each year following the year reported on (This form has recently been revised in 2009). The due date cannot be extended. The extensions filed for your tax returns do not extend the due date of this form. The address to file this return which is:

U.S. Department of the Treasury
P.O. Box 32621
Detroit, MI 48232USA

We are informed that the following street address can be used for DHL or Fed Exp delivery of the form in order to meet the deadline ,but please double check it before sending :

U.S. Department of Treasury, Currency Transaction Reporting,
985 Michigan Avenue
Detroit, Michigan 48226. USA

In recent testimony by Treasury Department officials, it was made clear that addressing the lack of disclosure of foreign financial accounts has become a priority. IRS has recently developed an Offshore Voluntary Compliance Initiative (OVCI) that allows partial amnesty until April 15, 2003. Also, new, easier to impose penalties, on top of those that already exist, are likely to be added by Congress this year for non-filing of the Treasury Form TD F 90-22.1. The Secretary of the Treasury may impose a civil penalty on any person who willfully violates this reporting requirement. The civil penalty is the amount of the transaction or the value of the account, up to a maximum of $100,000; the minimum amount of the penalty is $25,000. In addition, any person who willfully violates this reporting requirement is subject to a criminal penalty. The criminal penalty is a fine of not more than $250,000 or imprisonment for not more than five years (or both); if the violation is part of a pattern of illegal activity, the maximum amount of the fine is increased to $500,000 and the maximum length of imprisonment is increased to 10 years.

Congress in 2004 amended this section to provide that the Treasury can assess the a $10,000 penalty whether the failure to file this information form is willful or not. This penalty can be waived by the Treasury for reasonable cause if the return has been filed. The Treasury has not given any guidance on reasonable cause or on when it will or will not impose a penalty. Any form not filed is subject to the same penalty upon later discovery by the IRS. Therefore, it is best to attach an explanation with reasonable cause to any late filed TDF 90-221.

New FATCA Filing Requirements (*Foreign Account Taxpayer Compliance Act*)

In the wake of the US government's crackdown on undisclosed foreign bank accounts, the Internal Revenue Service has recently imposed additional reporting requirements that will obligate U.S. taxpayers to annually disclose specified foreign financial assets when they file their personal income tax returns for 2011 and thereafter.

The new foreign asset reporting rules, which are part of the Foreign Account Tax Compliance Act (FATCA), significantly expand the disclosure requirements well beyond what was previously required to be reported. The new Form 8938, Statement of Specified Foreign Financial Assets, requires individual taxpayers to report their interests in a wide variety of foreign assets. And yes, failure to file Form 8938 can result in substantial penalties as well as further government inquiry into a taxpayer's financial affairs. What makes this even more relevant is that the US Treasury Department earlier this year unveiled a groundbreaking agreement with France, Germany, Italy, Spain, and the UK to create an intergovernmental exchange of information on bank accounts held across borders. And just this past week the US Treasury said it reached agreements with both Switzerland and Japan to cooperate on a framework for sharing financial information on bank accounts.

While the winds of change are blowing, the proposed regulations are not final, and entities are generally not required to file Form 8938.

Foreign Asset Tax Compliance Act (FATCA) and required foreign asset reporting

The Form 8938 filing requirement is part of FATCA, which was enacted in 2010. It is intended to improve tax compliance by US taxpayers who hold offshore financial accounts.

Under FATCA, foreign financial institutions are required to report to the IRS certain information about the financial accounts held by US taxpayers or foreign entities in which US taxpayers hold a substantial ownership interest. Note that the new Offshore Voluntary Disclosure Initiative (OVDI) relates to Form TD F 90-22.1-refer to http://www.irs.gov/uac/2012-Offshore-Voluntary-Disclosure-Program) or to Report a Foreign Bank and/or Financial Accounts (FBAR), and that the Form 8938 filing requirement does not pre-empt the FBAR filing requirements.

Who should file form 8938?

Form 8938 is required to be filed by US citizens and resident aliens as well as nonresident aliens who make an election to be treated as resident aliens for US tax purposes. The requirement to file only exists if the aggregate value of their "specified foreign financial assets" exceeds certain thresholds. If you have employees or officers on international assignments (inbound or outbound), this filing may be applicable to them as well.

Penalties

It is important for taxpayers to determine whether they are subject to this new requirement because the law imposes significant penalties for failing to comply. The penalty for failure to file a Form 8938 is $10,000, with an additional penalty of up to $50,000 for continued failure to file after receiving IRS notification to file. A separate accuracy-related penalty of 40 percent applies to any understatement of tax attributable to undisclosed assets.

Definition of specified foreign financial asset

For purposes of the reporting requirement for individuals with foreign assets, a "specified foreign financial asset" is any financial account maintained by a foreign financial institution, and any of the following assets which are not held in an account maintained by a financial institution:

- any stock or security issued by a person other than a US person,
- any financial instrument or contract held for investment that has an issuer or counterparty that is other than a US person, and
- any interest in a foreign entity.

Please note that the following are not considered reportable:

- A financial account maintained by a US payer, such as a domestic branch of a foreign financial institution or a foreign branch of a US financial institution.

- A financial account that is maintained by a dealer or trader in securities or commodities if all of the holdings in the account are subject to the mark-to-market accounting rules for dealers in securities or an election under section 475(e) or (f) is made for all of the holdings in the account.
- If a specified foreign financial asset is reported on Form 3520, Form 3520-A, Form 5471, Form 8621, Form 8865, or Form 8891, that asset need not be reported on Form 8938. However, these specific forms need to be identified on Form 8938 (type of form and number of forms filed, etc.). Even if a specified foreign financial asset is reported on a form listed above, the value of the asset is included in determining whether the aggregate value of your specified foreign financial assets is more than the reporting threshold that applies to you.

Specific thresholds for filing Form 8938

- **Unmarried taxpayers living in the US**: The total value of specified foreign financial assets is more than $50,000 on the last day of the tax year or more than $75,000 at any time during the tax year.
- **Married taxpayers filing a joint income tax return and living in the US**: The total value of specified foreign financial assets is more than $100,000 on the last day of the tax year or more than $150,000 at any time during the tax year.
- **Married taxpayers filing separate income tax returns and living in the US**: The total value of specified foreign financial assets is more than $50,000 on the last day of the tax year or more than $75,000 at any time during the tax year.
- **Taxpayers living abroad filing a return other than a joint return**: The total value of specified foreign assets is more than $200,000 on the last day of the tax year or more than $300,000 at any time during the year; or
- **Taxpayers living abroad filing a joint return**: The total value of specified foreign asset is more than $400,000 on the last day of the tax year or more than $600,000 at any time during the year.

If you are part owner of a foreign corporation ,Foreign LLC ,or Foreign Partnership:

If you as a US Citizen and you own 10% or more of a foreign corporation (a corporation organized outside of the USA) you are obligated to filed Form 5471 each year with your personal tax return (or your business corporation or LLC tax return if that is the owner of the foreign corporation). On this form you must report the ownership of the corporation and other data. It also includes a balance sheet for the corporation and income and expense sheet for the current year for the corporation.

The return also must include data on transactions between you and the foreign corporation, original capital contributions, and other relevant data. That return is 4 pages and several other schedules are required which can make it a 6 or seven page return.

If you combined with other US taxpayers own more than 50% of actual or equitable interest in your foreign corporation, it is then defined as a Controlled Foreign Corporation (CFC), If it is a CFC, certain types of income (Subpart F income) may be taxed and flow through to the US shareholders and cause them to pay tax on that income on their US personal or business tax returns. The rules are complex with respect to determining the types of income of a CFC are subpart F income.

Certain types of income such as dividends, interest, rental income, insurance income, offshore shipping income and personal service income is treated as Subpart F income. Subpart F income whether distributed or not is taxable to the US shareholders personal return (or corporate return if a US corporation is the owner) in the year it occurs as ordinary income. However, the income in a Controlled corporation from other types of operating businesses such retail stores, factories, etc. that do not have operations in the US and do not purchase goods from a US affiliate of the business is not taxed to the Controlled Corporation shareholders until it is actual distributed to them.

Dividends paid to shareholders of Foreign Corporations sometimes are eligible for the reduced qualified dividend rate (same rate as capital gains) when paid from the foreign corporation that is located in a country with which the US has a tax treaty and not subpart F income from a Controlled Foreign Corporation.

You also must file Form 926 to report capital contributions to foreign corporations with your US tax return for the year you make those contributions.

Certain types of foreign corporations (the type varies by Country) have been identified by the IRS as eligible to elect, for US tax purposes only, to be treated as flow through entities. This means that if the election is made by filing the appropriate form with the IRS, all of the income and expenses of that foreign entity will flow through and be taxed on the income tax returns of the US shareholder in the same manner as US partnership and LLC income flows through and is taxed on the tax returns of the owners. This often is an advantage if most of the net income is distributed to the shareholders since it allows them to claim the foreign taxes paid by the foreign corporation as a foreign tax credit against their US income tax on that flow through income and partially or totally offset that us income tax.

If you own part of a foreign partnership, foreign LLC or Foreign Trust, you are also obligated to file special forms with your US tax return or you may incur substantial penalties of $10,000 or more for filing those forms late or not at all. The IRS is currently on a serious crusade to force all US taxpayers to report their foreign income or ownership of foreign business or investment entities. It is not advisable to ignore these rules due to the possible severe penalties you will incur if you are caught not complying with the law or filing those forms late.

As mentioned above, US citizens and residents, whether living abroad or in the US, are required to file a federal income tax return for any tax year in which gross income is equal to or greater than the applicable exemption amount and standard deduction. Generally, US taxpayers must report their worldwide income on their returns, and not just their US sourced income.

The IRS has the authority to impose significant penalties for the failure to file an income tax return and all required forms such as Forms 8938, Form **TD F 90-22**.1 unless the taxpayer can show that the failure was due to "reasonable cause" and not willful neglect.

Owning Real Estate in a Foreign Country

If you own real estate abroad the US income tax rules with respect to that property are almost the same as if the property were located in the US. On your U.S. tax return you would depreciate (with one exception, read below) the property and follow the same rules with respect to income and expenses as you would on a property located in the USA. Owning a property overseas by itself, does not require you to file any "special" forms ,however , some additional new forms may be required depending on your operation of the property and any foreign entities which may be used to hold title to the property ,more on this later.

If the property is your primary personal residence, and you live in it full time 2 out of the past five years you can claim the sale of personal residence gain exclusion on the property ($250,000 if single or $500,000) if married and pay no taxes so long as your gain is less than that amount just as you would in the US. However, if the real estate is a second home or rental property, you may not escape taxation on the sale of the property by using a tax free 1031 exchange. Foreign properties are not eligible under this code section.

If your foreign real estate is a rental property, the rental income and expenses must be reported on your Form 1040 using schedule E. The depreciable building portion of your tax basis in the property must be depreciated over a 40 year straight line period. Land cost is not depreciable. The fact the property does not produce a profit does not exempt you from putting it on your US tax return. You can offset any foreign income taxes paid on rental profits or profit on sale against your US tax on that same taxable gain.

If you maintain a tax domicile in a US state, you must also report this foreign rental property or take your deductions on your personal foreign real estate on your state tax return. States in general do not allow foreign tax credits. Rental income is not eligible for the foreign earned income exclusion.

In some countries such as Costa Rica, title to all real estate is held through a Costa Rican corporation. You must report you ownership in this foreign corporation as well and you foreign bank accounts if applicable under the rules governing form TDF 90-22.1

The following additional forms may be required if you own a foreign property depending on the manner title is held and how the property is operated:

- Form 5471- For foreign corporations with more than 10% US owners.
- Form TDF 90.22-1- To be filed if any time during the year you had signature authority or an ownership interest one or more foreign bank accounts, financial accounts, debit card accounts, which together had at any time during the year more than $10,000 in them (collectively)
- Form 3520 and 3520A -Filed if you are a grantor, grantee or in some way connected with a foreign trust
- Form 926-Filed when property is transferred to a foreign corporation.
- Form 8865 Filed for foreign partnerships
- Form 8858 - Filed or Foreign Disregarded Entities

Failure to file most of these forms can result in the IRS imposing severe penalties unless you can show "reasonable cause" which is often difficult to prove.

Social Security Agreements-for both "self-employed" and "employees"

The aim of all U.S." totalization" agreements is to eliminate dual Social Security coverage and taxation while maintaining the coverage of as many workers as possible under the system of the country where they are likely to have the greatest attachment, both while working and after retirement. Each agreement seeks to achieve this goal through a set of objective rules.

A general misconception about U.S. agreements is that they allow dually covered workers or their employers to elect the system to which they will contribute. This is not the case. The agreements, moreover, do not change the basic coverage provisions of the participating countries' Social Security laws-- such as those that define covered earnings or work. They simply exempt workers from coverage under the system of one country or the other when their work would otherwise be covered under both systems.

Since the late 1970's, the United States has established a network of bilateral Social Security agreements that coordinate the U.S. Social Security program with the comparable programs of other countries. Here is a brief overview of the agreements and should be of particular interest to multinational companies and to people who work abroad during their careers.

International Social Security agreements, often called "totalization agreements," have two main purposes. First, they eliminate dual Social Security taxation, the situation that occurs when a worker from one country works in another country and is required to pay Social Security taxes to both countries on the same earnings. Second, the agreements help fill gaps in benefit protection for workers who have divided their careers between the United States and another country.

Self Employment

U.S. Social Security coverage extends to self-employed U.S. citizens and residents whether their work is performed in the United States or another country. As a result, when they work outside the United States, citizens and residents are almost always dually covered since the host country will normally cover them also.

Most U.S. agreements eliminate dual coverage of self-employment by assigning coverage to the worker's country of residence. For example, under the U.S.-Swedish agreement, a dually covered self-employed U.S. citizen living in Sweden is covered only by the Swedish system and is excluded from U.S. coverage.

Although the agreements with Belgium, France, Germany, Italy and Japan do not use the residence rule as the primary determinant of self-employment coverage, each of them includes a provision to ensure that workers are covered and taxed in only one country. You can obtain more details on any of these agreements here on our web site or by writing to the Social Security Administration (SSA)

Agreements to coordinate Social Security protection across national boundaries have been common in Western Europe for decades. Following is a list of the agreements the United States has concluded and the date of the entry into force of each. Some of these agreements were subsequently revised; the date shown is the date the original agreement entered into force.

Countries with Social Security Agreements	
Country	*Entry into Force*
Italy	November 1, 1978
Germany	December 1, 1979
Switzerland	November 1, 1980
Belgium	July 1, 1984
Norway	July 1, 1984
Canada	August 1, 1984

United Kingdom	January 1, 1985
Sweden	January 1, 1987
Spain	April 1, 1988
France	July 1, 1988
Portugal	August 1, 1989
Netherlands	November 1, 1990
Austria	November 1, 1991
Finland	November 1, 1992
Ireland	September 1, 1993
Luxembourg	November 1, 1993
Greece	September 1, 1994
South Korea	April 1, 2001
Chile	December 1, 2001
Australia	October 1, 2002
Japan	October 1, 2005
Denmark	October 1, 2008
Czech Republic	January 1, 2009
Poland	March 1, 2009

The Problem of Dual Coverage

Without some means of coordinating Social Security coverage, people who work outside their country of origin may find themselves covered under the systems of two countries simultaneously for the same work. When this happens, both countries generally require the employer and employee or self-employed person to pay Social Security taxes.

Dual Social Security tax liability is a widespread problem for U.S. multinational companies and their employees because the U.S. Social Security program covers expatriate workers--those coming to the United States and those going abroad--to a greater extent than the programs of most other countries. U.S. Social Security extends to American citizens and U.S. resident aliens employed abroad by American employers without regard to the duration of an employee's foreign assignment, and even if the employee has been hired abroad. This extraterritorial U.S. coverage frequently results in dual tax liability for the employer and employee since most countries, as a rule, impose Social Security contributions on anyone working in their territory.

Dual tax liability can also affect U.S. citizens and residents working for foreign affiliates of American companies. This is likely to be the case when a U.S. firm has followed the common practice of entering into an agreement with the Department of the Treasury pursuant to section 3121(l) of the Internal Revenue Code to provide Social Security coverage for U.S. citizens and residents employed by the affiliate. In addition, U.S. citizens and residents who are self-employed outside the United States are often subject to dual Social Security tax liability since they remain covered under the U.S. program even if they maintain no business operations in the United States.

Other features of U.S. law increase the odds that foreign workers in the United States will also face dual coverage. U.S. law provides compulsory Social Security coverage for services performed in the United States as an employee, regardless of the citizenship or country of residence of the employee or employer, and irrespective of the length of time the employee stays in the United States. Unlike many other countries, the United States generally does not provide coverage exemptions for nonresident alien employees or for employees who have been sent to work within its borders for short periods. For this reason, most foreign workers in the United States are covered under the U.S. program.

Paying dual Social Security contributions is especially costly for companies that offer "tax equalization" arrangements for their expatriate employees. A firm that sends an employee to work in another country often guarantees that the assignment will not result in a reduction of the employee's after-tax income. Employers with tax equalization programs, therefore, typically agree to pay both the employer and employee share of host country Social Security taxes on behalf of their transferred employees.

Under the tax laws of many countries, however, an employer's payment of an employee's share of a Social Security contribution is considered to be taxable compensation to the employee, thus increasing the employee's income tax liability. The tax equalization arrangement generally provides that the employer will also pay this additional income tax, which in turn serves to increase the employee's taxable income and tax liability even further. The employer again pays the additional tax, etc., etc.

Requesting Certificates of Coverage or Exemption from Social Security Taxes

Workers who are exempt from U.S. or foreign Social Security taxes under an agreement must document their exemption by obtaining a certificate of coverage from the country that will continue to cover them. For example, a U.S. worker sent on temporary assignment to the United Kingdom would need a certificate of coverage issued by SSA to prove his or her exemption from U.K. Social Security contributions. Conversely, a U.K.-based employee working temporarily in the United States would need a certificate from the U.K. authorities as evidence of the exemption from U.S. Social Security tax.

When SSA issues a certificate certifying U.S. coverage, a copy of the certificate usually must be presented to the appropriate foreign authorities as proof of entitlement to the foreign exemption for the U.S. employee and the employer. When the other country issues a certificate certifying that the employee is covered by the foreign system, the employer can immediately stop withholding and paying U.S. Social Security taxes on the employee's earnings. The certificate should just be retained in the employer's files so it can be produced in the event the Internal Revenue Service ever questions why no taxes are being paid for the employee. A self-employed U.S. citizen or resident must attach a photocopy of the foreign certificate to his U.S. tax return each year as proof of the U.S. exemption from self-employment taxes. In accordance with Revenue Procedure 84-54, the foreign certificate serves as proof of the exemption from U.S. Social Security taxes for the period shown on the certificate.

Employers generally are required to request certificates on behalf of employees they have transferred abroad; self-employed persons request their own certificate. Certificates of U.S. coverage may be requested by writing to the address at the end of this article.

Requests should include the employer's name and address in the United States and the other country, the worker's full name, place and date of birth, citizenship, U.S. and foreign Social Security numbers, place and date of hiring, and the beginning and ending dates of the assignment in the foreign country. (If the employee will be working for a foreign affiliate of the U.S. company, the request should also indicate whether U.S. Social Security coverage has been arranged for the employees of the affiliate under section 3121(l) of the Internal Revenue Code.) Self-employed persons should indicate their country of residence and the nature of their self-employment activity. When requesting certificates under the agreements with France and Japan, the employer (or self-employed person) must also indicate whether the worker and any accompanying family members are covered by health insurance.

(N.B. The provisions for eliminating dual coverage apply to coverage and contributions under the U.S. retirement, survivors, disability and hospital (Medicare) insurance programs, and the retirement, survivors and disability insurance programs in the foreign countries. Some agreements may also apply to coverage and contributions under additional programs in the foreign country, such as insurance for short-term sickness, work accident and unemployment. As a result, workers exempted from foreign coverage by one of these agreements pay no Social Security taxes for these additional programs and generally may not receive benefits from them. In this case, the worker and employer

As one can readily see, the employee's foreign Social Security coverage results in a substantially greater tax burden for the employer than the nominal Social Security tax alone. Depending on the other country's tax rates, in some countries this "pyramid" effect has been known to increase an employer's foreign Social Security costs to as much as 65-70 percent of the employee's salary.

International Social Security agreements are advantageous both for persons who are working now and for those whose working careers are over. For current workers, the agreements eliminate the dual contributions they might otherwise be paying to the Social Security systems of both the United States and another country. For persons who have worked both in the United States and abroad, and who are now retired, disabled, or deceased, the agreements often result in the payment of benefits to which the worker or the worker's family members would not otherwise have become entitled.

The agreements also favorably affect the profitability and competitive position of companies with foreign operations by reducing their cost of doing business abroad. Companies with personnel stationed abroad are encouraged to take advantage of these agreements to reduce their tax burden.

Anyone who would like more information about the United States' Social Security "totalization" agreements program--including details about specific agreements that are in force--should write to:

SOCIAL SECURITY ADMINISTRATION
Office of International Programs
P.O. Box 17741
Baltimore, Maryland 21235-7741
USA

You can also write to the address above if you would like to suggest the negotiation of new agreements with specific countries. In developing its negotiating plans, SSA gives considerable weight to the interest expressed by the workers and employers who will be affected by potential agreements.

In Summary

Stay in compliance, the IRS is on the lookout for Americans living overseas who have not filed their returns or reported their foreign "worldwide" holdings on a timely fashion. Ignorance is not an excuse but in some cases the IRS will give you a break if you can prove a "reasonable cause", you don't owe a lot to the IRS and fail to file was not due to "willful neglect". To claim this exception you need to write , "filed pursuant to section 1.911 " - read the section on **Electing The Exclusion** above on page 10 and the IRS will decide if they will grant you that exclusion. Generally speaking the IRS will look back 6 years if you have not filed a return for several years while living overseas but filing a return for every year is still required and they, the IRS can go back as far as they wish. If you are due a refund you will only be able to claim it for 2 years from the filing date, plus extensions on your tax return.
Living overseas is exciting and fun but adding extra drama or stress is not needed.

I have personally prepared over 10,000 US tax returns over the past 30 years and I have seen almost every type of tax situation. If you want assistance in preparing your return for 2012 or prior years, please fill out the following questionnaire in part II and send back to me. If you paid for this booklet and you want me to prepare your return I will deduct $25 from your tax preparation fee. My email address is CPrice@HRBlock.com, my telephone number is USA 206-935-2163, fax number is USA 206-770-7586.

Best wishes and good luck!

Part II

EXPATRIATE TAX QUESTIONNAIRE FOR U.S. CITIZENS LIVING ABROAD

This questionnaire can be filled out by hand or in MS Word

Indicate year this form is completed for - if not 2012: _____

	Primary Taxpayer	Spouse (write N/A if not married name)
Name	_____	_____
Social Security Number	_____	_____
Date of Birth	_____	_____
Profession	_____	_____
Citizenship Country	_____	_____
U.S. Green Card Holder?	_____	_____

Indicate if Green Card obtained or relinquished this year and date

Did you file a joint U.S. return with your spouse last year? _____ Yes _____ No _____N/A
Did your marital status change this year? _____ Yes _____ No _____N/A
Indicate any U.S. States where you filed a tax return last year: _____
Might you be required to file a tax return with a US state as well? ____Yes____ No _____Don't know
        -Please Explain._____

Contact Information

Email Address(es)   _____

Phone Numbers (indicate home,
office, or mobile)   _____

Residence Address in Foreign Country

_____

_____

Mailing Address to be shown on Tax Return:

_____

_____

If a U.S. address, please indicate c/o and Name if mail is going to someone else

Best time or method to contact _____

Dependent Children's Names, Gender of Child, Dates of Birth, and Social Security Numbers and if a US citizen:

Please note if your children are <u>not U.S. citizens</u> please state their country of citizenship. Also please note if your children have earned income, investment income, are married, or are not residing with you as the custodial parent. Also indicate if you have dependents other than children that are U.S. citizens or residents. Attach extra sheet for answers if needed.

1. Date you arrived to live & work in your foreign residence country: _____

2. Are you still a resident of the Foreign Country?   _____ Yes   _____ No

3. If not, what date did you return to the U.S. to take up residency and
    to which state did you move?_____

4. If you have previously filed Form 2555/2555EZ (foreign earned income
    exclusion) with your return, what was the last year you filed this form?   _____

If you were present in the U.S. or U.S. possessions during the calendar year in question, please fill in the following information for each trip to the U.S. (attach additional sheet if necessary):

Date Arrived in U.S.	Date Departed U.S.	Income Earned in U.S. (indicate which state)	Employer's Name
		$ _____State	
		$ _____ State	
		$ _____ State	

If you moved to or from the U.S. this year you may need to qualify under a 330 day physical presence test. In that case, we need a schedule of all U.S. trips through today's date

NOTE: You can use www.oanda.com/currency **for historical currency conversions (typically average exchange rate for the year is used).**

PRIMARY TAXPAYER EARNED INCOME INFORMATION:

5. Employer's Name and Address: _____

6. Employer's U.S. office address (if any): _____

7. Employer is a ____Foreign Company _____ U.S. Company _____Foreign Subsidiary of a U.S. Company

8. Gross wages/salary earned in foreign country for calendar year in US Dollars: _____

9. Foreign Income Taxes paid for Calendar tax year on your salary in US Dollars: _____

10. Indicate currency in which foreign wages/taxes are paid and exchange rate you used: _____

11. If applicable, is all income on a Form W-2 issued by a U.S. company? _____Yes _____ No

SPOUSE'S EARNED INCOME INFORMATION:

12. Employer's Name and Address: _____

13. Employer's U.S. office address (if any): _____

14. Employer is a ____Foreign Company _____ U.S. Company _____Foreign Subsidiary of a U.S. Company

15. Gross wages/salary earned in foreign country for calendar year in US Dollars: _____

16. Foreign Income Taxes paid for Calendar tax year on your salary in US Dollars: _____

17. Indicate currency in which foreign wages/taxes are paid and exchange rate you used: _____

18. If applicable, is all income on a Form W-2 issued by a U.S. company? _____Yes _____ No

NOTE: In some countries (U.K., Australia, Hong Kong) the normal tax year is a fiscal year (such as April 6 to April 5). However, all income, deductions, and tax credits must be reported on a <u>Calendar Year Basis</u> (Jan 1 to Dec 31). Therefore it may be necessary to adjust your foreign fiscal year income/taxes from your foreign tax return to the correct calendar year amount acceptable by the IRS.

IMPORTANT: There is no foreign income exclusion allowed for calculating Self Employment Taxes (FICA/Medicare) – unless you live in a country that has a Social Security Agreement/Treaty with the U.S. (Approx 20 countries) and you are paying the equivalent social security tax in that country. If applicable, a certificate from that country showing payment compliance may be required. If self-employed you will owe the U.S. self-employment social security tax on your net business income (up to 15.3%) unless you are covered by the social security agreement/treaty in your country of residence.

19. Were you or your spouse **self-employed** or **independent contractors** in the foreign country?	_____ Yes _____ No
20. Type of Business	
21. Business Name	
22. EIN Number, if any (US ID number)	
23. Ownership	____ Husband ____ Wife ____ Joint

If self-employed in business, please complete a statement of income and <u>itemized expenses</u> for the business for this calendar year and attach the statement to this packet. You may request our self-employment questionnaire supplement). List totals below:

24. Total gross business income for tax year in USD	$
25. Total business expenses for tax year in USD	$

26. Do you rent or own your residence overseas, or is it provided by employer? ____ Rent ____ Own
_____Provided by Employer

27. If employer provided housing, amount paid by employer: $_____. Is this housing amount already included in the income you provided in question #8? _____Yes _____No

28. Rent and Utilities paid on foreign residence, other than telephone: _____

29. Indicate family members living with you overseas and for what period:

_____

30. Are you required to pay income taxes in the foreign country? _____ Yes _____ No

31. What type of Visa do you hold for your resident country?_____

US EMPLOYMENT EARNED INCOME: If you moved to a foreign country during this year or moved back to the U.S. during this tax year please complete this question relating to your period of <u>U.S. employment</u>:

32. Employer Name and Address (if self-employed indicate and attach a list of income/expense for the U.S. period of time): _____

33. Occupation: _____

34. Income: _____

35. Period of time working for this employer: _____

36. W-2 attached? (provide W-2 breakdown if available)_____ _____

RENTAL INCOME AND EXPENSES

If you own rental property in the U.S. or abroad, please attach a sheet showing all income and summarized expenses for the year. If we did not do your return last year, we will also need the date the rental began, amount paid for property, amount allocable to land, any major improvements, and a copy of the previous depreciation schedule if previously depreciated. (Ask us for a rental property questionnaire if you need to give us this data and it will be e-mailed to you).

Indicate how many properties you have rented out or had available for rent this tax year, if any. Please provide locations of properties and describe the rental activities.	

37. Do you maintain a U.S. home while living abroad? If so, provide address: _____ Yes _____ No

_____

38. If your U.S. residence is occupied indicate who is living in the residence, their relation, and whether this residence is rented: _____

_____

NON-EARNED INCOME (Attach separate sheets if additional space needed for any items)

Interest Income (Indicate currency if not listed in USD):

Description/Payor	Location of Payor if not U.S.	Ordinary Interest	Tax Free Interest	Foreign Taxes Paid
		$	$	$
		$	$	$
		$	$	$

Dividend Income (Indicate currency if not listed in USD):

Description/Payor	Location of Payor if not U.S.	Ordinary Dividend	Qualified Portion	Capital Gain Distribution
		$	$	$
		$	$	$
		$	$	$

If there were foreign taxes withheld from any please provide further information.

Capital Gain Income (Stock or property sales – include any statements):

Description	Country	Date acquired	Date Sold	Sales price	Original cost plus purchase fees
				$	$
				$	$
				$	$

31

If there were foreign taxes paid on or U.S. taxes withheld from these transactions let us know. Also ensure you have indicated the currency accurately if not U.S. Dollars. <u>Please provide us with the realized gain/loss report from your broker.</u>

<u>Other Income</u> (for instance, director's fees, retirement, social security, alimony, debt forgiveness, gambling winnings, etc.):

Description/Payor	Location of other income	Amount of income	Explanation
		$	
		$	

Please indicate if you sold your principal residence/former principal residence this year _____Yes ___ No

DEDUCTIONS

Describe deductions, the amounts paid, and dates paid. If a deduction does not apply to you, you can leave blank or indicate N/A.

39. Medical and Dental Expenses (please note these need to exceed 7.5% of gross Income to receive any benefit). You may also include medical/dental insurance premiums. US$_____

40. Interest on Home Mortgage in USA (please advise if you have mortgages on more than 2 homes). US$_____

41. Interest on Mortgage outside the US (state name and address of entity to which you paid foreign mortgage payments). Also indicate currency: _____

42. Interest on any other mortgage such as a "second mortgage/home equity loan":

43. _____ Yes _____ No
Please describe:_____

44. Indicate if you refinanced a mortgage this year: _____ Yes _____ No

45. Auto License Fees   US$_____

46. Sales Tax paid to a U.S. state – if any (this generally only applies to residents in a no income tax state):
                                                                US$_____

47. Property Taxes on U.S. property (indicate which property if more than one): Please provide copy of property tax bill if a California property. US$_____

48. Property Taxes on Foreign property (describe property): US$_____

49. U.S. Charitable contributions to U.S. Charities - only for which you have proper documentation (provide detailed information about donations):
_____

50. Investment Interest Expenses (such as a margin loan):   US$_____

51. Other Investment Expenses (describe): US$_____

52. Tax Preparation Fees paid during the tax year   US$_____

53. Provide Details of any moving or storage expenses:_____

54. Interest on Student Loans (indicate who for) _____

55. Tuition and other Educational expenses (provide details): _____

OTHER QUESTIONS/INFORMATION

56. Foreign Taxes paid on income other than wages such as on foreign interest, dividends, rents, royalties, etc. – this does not include VAT. _____

57. Rolled over foreign tax credits from previous years (OR provide
schedule from prior year return)
_____

58. Do you file a non-resident state return in any state? If so, why?
_____

59. Was any of your income received this year from stock options, deferred compensation plans, or other executive
plans?_____

60. Are you covered by a foreign pension plan (not U.S. qualified)? Contributions may be taxable, or require
additional special reporting forms each year._____

61. Investments in a foreign mutual fund (not traded on the U.S. stock market) can be subject to a very complicated
and adverse tax calculation in the U.S. It is important we are notified of these investments so we can do the
required calculations. Do you have investments in foreign mutual funds which are not part of your US
brokerage account?   _____Yes   _____No

62. Do you make contributions to any retirement plan (other than   _____ I make contributions
401(k)) or want to? Are you interested in converting to a ROTH   _____ I do not make contributions
IRA, if eligible?   Check all that apply and provide relevant   _____ My spouse contributes
information   _____I am interested in making
                                                                       contributions
                                                                       _____ I am interested in converting to
                                                                       a ROTH

63. Do you want to have any tax refund directly deposited into your   _____ Name of Bank
U.S. checking or savings account? If so, please provide the   _____ Routing # (9 digit
following banking information. In certain cases your tax balance   number on bottom left of check)
due (if any) can be automatically withdrawn from your bank   _____ Acct Number
account when we e-file your return and only **after** you return   ____ Checking ____Savings
your authorization form confirming your agreement of tax due. If
you are interested in electronic payment of tax due check here

____

64. Did you make any quarterly estimated tax payments for federal or state? If so, please provide
details:_____

65. Please list any other items of income or expense that you feel might affect your U.S. taxes, or any other
information you want to provide:
_____
_____
_____

IMPORTANT - ADDITIONAL FORMS WHICH MAY BE REQUIRED

A. The IRS requires special forms be filed by any U.S. Taxpayer who owns all or part of a foreign corporation,
foreign LLC (or equivalent), foreign LLP, foreign partnership, or foreign trust (such as a fideicomiso in
Mexico). If you fail to file these forms, you will be subject to substantial penalties if it is ever discovered that
you should have filed those forms. Please indicate here if you are an owner of a foreign corporation or trust and
we will send you an additional questionnaire for the information required to be reported in those forms.
Yes _____   No _____   If Yes, please describe: _____

B. FOREIGN FINANCIAL ASSET REPORTING REQUIREMENT: There is a new reporting requirement (first
instituted for the 2011 tax year) for individuals who have "Specified Foreign Financial Assets" in excess of
certain levels. Specified Foreign Financial assets include the following:
   • Deposit or Custodial accounts (such as bank accounts) at a foreign financial institution, including
     certain retirement accounts
   • Any equity or debt interest in a foreign financial institution

- Other foreign investments such as stock issued by non-US persons, any interest in a foreign entity, and any financial instrument issued by a non-US person.
- Foreign real estate is NOT a specified foreign financial asset and you do not have to count it, unless it is a Mexican property in a fideicomiso.

IF YOUR TOTAL FOREIGN FINANCIAL ASSETS (INCLUDING FOREIGN BANK ACCOUNTS) EXCEED THE FOLLOWING LEVELS THIS FORM IS REQUIRED:

Filing Situation	Value on last day of the tax year is at least this amount:	Or, at any time during the tax year, the value is greater than:
Single or Married Filing Separate taxpayers living in the U.S.	$50,000	$75,000
Married Taxpayers filing jointly living in the U.S.	$100,000	$150,000
Taxpayers not filing jointly who are living outside the U.S. and would qualify for the foreign earned income exclusion	$200,000	$300,000
Married Taxpayers filing jointly who are living abroad and would qualify for the foreign earned income exclusion	$400,000	$600,000

This new requirement **does not** replace the foreign bank account filing requirement (described below). This is an **additional** requirement. If you are subject to this requirement we may contact you for additional information. There can be severe civil and criminal penalties for non-filing of this form if necessary. This form is not required for tax years before 2011.

Based on the above, do you have a requirement to file this form? Check one of the following:

_____ Yes   _____No   _____I am not sure, contact me to discuss.

Please explain: _____

If your only specified foreign financial assets are foreign bank or custodial accounts check here: _____ and complete the foreign bank account section below.

C. Are you a signatory on a foreign bank account, foreign investment account, or other foreign account whether you are the owner or not? _____ Yes _____ No

D. Did you have an ownership interest in a foreign bank account, and did the total amount in all of your foreign bank and other financial accounts ever equal or exceed the equivalent of US $10,000 at any point during this tax year? ___ Yes ____ No If yes, please complete the following information:

NOTE: Questions B and C relate to the Treasury form TDF 90.22-1 which requires reporting of foreign bank accounts. **This form is filed separately from your tax return and you can complete it on your own.** This form must be received by the authorities no later than June 30th or you may incur severe penalties. **No extensions are available beyond that due date for this form. The form can be found at:**
http://www.irs.gov/pub/irs-pdf/f90221.pdf
If you choose to prepare this form on your own check here _____ and provide us a copy when complete. If you would like us to complete the form for you, please fill in the information below:

Name of Bank or Institution   _____

Address of Bank incl. City, Country, Postcode   _____

Account Number   _____

Country of Account Location   _____

34

Highest balance of account in USD during tax year
(exchange rate to be used is as of Dec 31)   _____

Type of Account (securities, bank, pension)   _____

Indicate if spouse is co-owner **or** list name, address,
and SSN of co-owner if not spouse   _____

Name of owner of account if you only sign on the
account and are not an owner.   _____

If you are subject to the specified foreign financial requirement described in B above, we also need to know the following for each account:

Indicate if account opened or closed this year   Opened _____ Closed _____

Highest value during the year in foreign currency
(indicate currency)   _____

Please attach additional sheets with the above information for each of your foreign bank accounts, foreign savings accounts, foreign stock or financial accounts (this includes credit card accounts with credit balances). Foreign mortgage accounts are not subject to this requirement. You may also request we send you our foreign account questionnaire which allows for more accounts to be listed. Make sure to include all interest/dividend and other income from these accounts in the appropriate section of the questionnaire.

Please attach a copy of all W-2's and/or any 1099's received from U.S. employers or banking or investment accounts. Also, if we did not prepare your return last year, please send us a copy of last years' state and federal tax returns – preferably by e-mail attachment or fax, but if too lengthy then a copy by mail. Do not send originals of any forms! **We will not be responsible for their maintenance or return to you.**

HAVE QUESTIONS OR NEED FURTHER INFORMATION?

Our main U.S. phone number is 206-935-2163. Secure e-faxes can be sent to (206) 770-7586. Scheduled calls are also available on Skype, my Skype name is: cbprice1.

GENERAL INFORMATION AND IMPORTANT DUE DATES

Expatriates (U.S. citizens living abroad on April 15) are given an automatic extension to file their tax return until June 15- it is best to write "Taxpayer living overseas on June 15th" on top of the return to get the attention of the IRS, however, if any taxes are owed, the money is due on April 15 if you wish to avoid possible penalties and interest. A further extension for filing of tax returns until October 15 may be obtained by filing the proper extension form by June 15. *If your return needs to be completed by April 15, we recommend your questionnaire be submitted to us no later than March 18.* We can prepare an extension for you at no charge.

The Treasury form reporting foreign bank accounts must be received by the authorities no later than June 30 or you may incur severe penalties. **No extensions are available beyond that due date for this form.**
If you own part of a foreign corporation, foreign partnership, for foreign LLC (or equivalent), the special IRS tax forms required for those entities are due on the same dates as your personal tax return, including any extension. If there is a foreign trust, such as a Mexican Fideicomiso, the IRS tax return form 3520A is due on March 15th, and the 3520 form, if required, is due with the personal tax return. If you received a gift/bequest greater than $100,000 from a non-U.S. Person or estate, if you received a gift from non-U.S. corporations or partnerships in excess of US $14,723, or if you gifted more than $13,000 to any one person, an additional filing may be required separate from your tax return.

The Internal Revenue Service requires tax returns be filed for every year, even if you owe no taxes due to foreign tax credits or the foreign earned income exclusion! The foreign earned income exclusion can only be claimed if you file a tax return and meet the IRS requirements for physical presence or bona fide residence.

The IRS will currently accept late filed returns and still allow the foreign earned income exemption subject to the taxes owed with that return – though this is subject to change in the future. **NOTE:** If you are submitting delinquent foreign bank account forms, delinquent forms 8938, delinquent foreign corporation or partnership forms, or delinquent foreign trust forms, we recommend you have a consultation about the Offshore Voluntary Disclosure Program (http://www.irs.gov/uac/2012-Offshore-Voluntary-Disclosure-Program) **or**, if you are eligible, the IRS Streamlined Procedure (http://www.irs.gov/uac/Instructions-for-New-Streamlined-Filing-Compliance-Procedures-for-Non-Resident-Non-Filer-US-Taxpayers). If you submit these delinquent forms outside this program or procedure you may be subject to more stringent penalties and/or prosecution.

The undersigned taxpayer(s) hereby engage the accounting offices of Christopher B Price, Inc DBA H&R Block, to prepare **2012** &_____ (list other years if they are involved) U.S. Federal and or state tax returns. If we are engaging you to prepare foreign related delinquent forms, we acknowledge notification regarding the potential penalties for late filing of these forms and acknowledge notification regarding the Offshore Voluntary Disclosure Program (if applicable).

In connection with that preparation we understand that it is my (our) obligation to provide complete and accurate information on all items of income and deductions for the tax year(s) involved and I/(we) are responsible for any omissions. All information stated in the questionnaire is true and correct and we accept sole responsibility for any inaccuracies or information not disclosed to the tax return preparer in writing.

We have receipts and other written documents to support all of the information provided. We will retain these records for a period of at least ten years after the date the returns are filed in the event of a tax audit. Preparers do not save copies of the documentation given in connection with the return preparation. We understand that Preparers have no obligation to verify or confirm the information we provide and that we are responsible for its completeness and accuracy. We understand that our file will only be retained by Preparers office for five years from the date the service is rendered and will then be destroyed.

We also understand that the cost of preparing our tax returns is dependent on the completeness of the data we supply to Preparers and the complexity and number of various tax forms, calculations and schedules that must, by law, be included in our returns. The cost of the preparation of the return/s will increase above the fee originally quoted if data received is more complex than originally provided/described, is incomplete, or if additional time must be spent sorting through source documents not summarized by the taxpayer. We agree to this fee increase in advance and acknowledge it is possible.

those matters. Any representation before tax agencies for audits or other matters will be subject to extra fees.

We further represent that if we instructed you that our foreign earned income should not be shown on Schedule C as self-employed, that we have represented to Preparers that we are bona fide employees of a foreign employer and subject to foreign income tax withholding and a social security equivalent. We accept full responsibility for documenting and proving this fact in the event we are audited by the IRS. We understand that if we are independent contractors, we must pay up to 15.3% U.S. self-employment tax on our foreign earned income after deducting all applicable business expenses. Preparers are not responsible for any penalties, interest or taxes resulting from our failure to properly show us as self-employed.

IN WITNESS WHEREOF, this agreement is executed on the dates first stated below:

Taxpayer Signature: _____   Spouse Signature: _____
                    Typing your name above is deemed to be a signature, for instance if you do not have access

to a scanner

Date Signed: _____   Date Signed: _____

NOTICE: This questionnaire and/or e-mail (and any attachments) is confidential and proprietary. It is for the sole use of the intended recipient(s) and any use or disclosure by others is prohibited.

Part III

Form 926

Form **926**
(Rev. December 2011)
Department of the Treasury
Internal Revenue Service

Return by a U.S. Transferor of Property to a Foreign Corporation

▶ Attach to your income tax return for the year of the transfer or distribution.

OMB No. 1545-0026

Attachment
Sequence No. **128**

Part I U.S. Transferor Information (see instructions)

Name of transferor | Identifying number (see instructions)

1 If the transferor was a corporation, complete questions 1a through 1d.

a If the transfer was a section 361(a) or (b) transfer, was the transferor controlled (under section 368(c)) by 5 or fewer domestic corporations? . . . . ☐ Yes ☐ No

b Did the transferor remain in existence after the transfer? . . . . ☐ Yes ☐ No

If not, list the controlling shareholder(s) and their identifying number(s):

Controlling shareholder	Identifying number

c If the transferor was a member of an affiliated group filing a consolidated return, was it the parent corporation? . . . . ☐ Yes ☐ No

If not, list the name and employer identification number (EIN) of the parent corporation:

Name of parent corporation	EIN of parent corporation

d Have basis adjustments under section 367(a)(5) been made? . . . . ☐ Yes ☐ No

2 If the transferor was a partner in a partnership that was the actual transferor (but is not treated as such under section 367), complete questions 2a through 2d.

a List the name and EIN of the transferor's partnership:

Name of partnership	EIN of partnership

b Did the partner pick up its pro rata share of gain on the transfer of partnership assets? . . . . ☐ Yes ☐ No
c Is the partner disposing of its **entire** interest in the partnership? . . . . ☐ Yes ☐ No
d Is the partner disposing of an interest in a limited partnership that is regularly traded on an established securities market? . . . . ☐ Yes ☐ No

Part II Transferee Foreign Corporation Information (see instructions)

3 Name of transferee (foreign corporation) | **4 Identifying number**, if any

5 Address (including country)

6 Country code of country of incorporation or organization (see instructions)

7 Foreign law characterization (see instructions)

8 Is the transferee foreign corporation a controlled foreign corporation? . . . . ☐ Yes ☐ No

For Paperwork Reduction Act Notice, see separate instructions. | Cat. No. 16982D | Form **926** (Rev. 12-2011)

38

Part III **Information Regarding Transfer of Property** (see instructions)

Type of property	(a) Date of transfer	(b) Description of property	(c) Fair market value on date of transfer	(d) Cost or other basis	(e) Gain recognized on transfer
Cash					
Stock and securities					
Installment obligations, account receivables or similar property					
Foreign currency or other property denominated in foreign currency					
Inventory					
Assets subject to depreciation recapture (see Temp. Regs. sec. 1.367(a)-4T(b))					
Tangible property used in trade or business not listed under another category					
Intangible property					
Property to be leased (as described in final and temp. Regs. sec. 1.367(a)-4(c))					
Property to be sold (as described in Temp. Regs. sec. 1.367(a)-4T(d))					
Transfers of oil and gas working interests (as described in Temp. Regs. sec. 1.367(a)-4T(e))					
Other property					

Supplemental Information Required To Be Reported (see instructions):

_____

_____

_____

_____

_____

Form **926** (Rev. 12-2011)

Part IV   **Additional Information Regarding Transfer of Property** (see instructions)

9   Enter the transferor's interest in the foreign transferee corporation before and after the transfer:

(a) Before _____ % (b) After _____ %

10   Type of nonrecognition transaction (see instructions) ▶ _____

11   Indicate whether any transfer reported in Part III is subject to any of the following:
a   Gain recognition under section 904(f)(3) . . . . ☐ Yes ☐ No
b   Gain recognition under section 904(f)(5)(F) . . . . ☐ Yes ☐ No
c   Recapture under section 1503(d) . . . . ☐ Yes ☐ No
d   Exchange gain under section 987 . . . . ☐ Yes ☐ No

12   Did this transfer result from a change in the classification of the transferee to that of a foreign corporation? ☐ Yes ☐ No
13   Indicate whether the transferor was required to recognize income under final and temporary Regulations sections 1.367(a)-4 through 1.367(a)-6 for any of the following:
a   Tainted property . . . . ☐ Yes ☐ No
b   Depreciation recapture . . . . ☐ Yes ☐ No
c   Branch loss recapture . . . . ☐ Yes ☐ No
d   Any other income recognition provision contained in the above-referenced regulations . . . . ☐ Yes ☐ No

14   Did the transferor transfer assets which qualify for the trade or business exception under section 367(a)(3)? ☐ Yes ☐ No

15a   Did the transferor transfer foreign goodwill or going concern value as defined in Temporary Regulations section 1.367(a)-1T(d)(5)(iii)? . . . . ☐ Yes ☐ No

b   If the answer to line 15a is "Yes," enter the amount of foreign goodwill or going concern value transferred ▶ $ _____

16   Was cash the only property transferred? . . . . ☐ Yes ☐ No

17a   Was intangible property (within the meaning of section 936(h)(3)(B)) transferred as a result of the transaction? . . . . ☐ Yes ☐ No

b   If "Yes," describe the nature of the rights to the intangible property that was transferred as a result of the transaction:

_____
_____
_____
_____

Form **926** (Rev. 12-2011)

Form 1116

Form 1116

Department of the Treasury
Internal Revenue Service (99)

Foreign Tax Credit

(Individual, Estate, or Trust)

▶ Attach to Form 1040, 1040NR, 1041, or 990-T.
▶ Information about Form 1116 and its separate instructions is at *www.irs.gov/form1116.*

OMB No. 1545-0121

2012

Attachment
Sequence No. **19**

Name	**Identifying number** as shown on page 1 of your tax return

Use a separate Form 1116 for each category of income listed below. See **Categories of Income** in the instructions. Check only one box on each Form 1116. Report all amounts in U.S. dollars except where specified in Part II below.

a ☐ Passive category income   **c** ☐ Section 901(j) income   **e** ☐ Lump-sum distributions

b ☐ General category income   **d** ☐ Certain income re-sourced by treaty

f Resident of (name of country) ▶

Note: *If you paid taxes to only one foreign country or U.S. possession, use column A in Part I and line A in Part II. If you paid taxes to* **more than one** *foreign country or U.S. possession, use a separate column and line for each country or possession.*

Part I — Taxable Income or Loss From Sources Outside the United States (for Category Checked Above)

		Foreign Country or U.S. Possession			Total (Add cols. A, B, and C.)
		A	B	C	
g	Enter the name of the foreign country or U.S. possession ▶				
1a	Gross income from sources within country shown above and of the type checked above (see instructions): _____ _____ _____				**1a**
b	Check if line 1a is compensation for personal services as an employee, your total compensation from all sources is $250,000 or more, and you used an alternative basis to determine its source (see instructions) . . ▶ ☐				
Deductions and losses (*Caution: See instructions*):					
2	Expenses **definitely related** to the income on line 1a (attach statement)				
3	Pro rata share of other deductions **not definitely related:**				
a	Certain itemized deductions or standard deduction (see instructions)				
b	Other deductions (attach statement)				
c	Add lines 3a and 3b				
d	Gross foreign source income (see instructions) .				
e	Gross income from all sources (see instructions) .				
f	Divide line 3d by line 3e (see instructions) . . .				
g	Multiply line 3c by line 3f				
4	Pro rata share of interest expense (see instructions):				
a	Home mortgage interest (use the Worksheet for Home Mortgage Interest in the instructions) . .				
b	Other interest expense				
5	Losses from foreign sources				
6	Add lines 2, 3g, 4a, 4b, and 5				**6**
7	Subtract line 6 from line 1a. Enter the result here and on line 15, page 2 . . . . ▶				**7**

Part II — Foreign Taxes Paid or Accrued (see instructions)

Country	Credit is claimed for taxes (you must check one)		Foreign taxes paid or accrued								
			In foreign currency				In U.S. dollars				
	(h) ☐ Paid		Taxes withheld at source on:			**(n)** Other foreign taxes paid or accrued	Taxes withheld at source on:			**(r)** Other foreign taxes paid or accrued	**(s)** Total foreign taxes paid or accrued (add cols. (o) through (r))
	(i) ☐ Accrued		**(k)** Dividends	**(l)** Rents and royalties	**(m)** Interest		**(o)** Dividends	**(p)** Rents and royalties	**(q)** Interest		
	(j) Date paid or accrued										
A											
B											
C											
8	Add lines A through C, column (s). Enter the total here and on line 9, page 2 . . . . ▶									**8**	

For Paperwork Reduction Act Notice, see instructions.   Cat. No. 11440U   Form **1116** (2012)

Part III Figuring the Credit

9	Enter the amount from line 8. These are your total foreign taxes paid or accrued for the category of income checked above Part I	9	
10	Carryback or carryover (attach detailed computation)	10	
11	Add lines 9 and 10	11	
12	Reduction in foreign taxes (see instructions)	12	( )
13	Taxes reclassified under high tax kickout (see instructions)	13	
14	Combine lines 11, 12, and 13. This is the total amount of foreign taxes available for credit		14
15	Enter the amount from line 7. This is your taxable income or (loss) from sources outside the United States (before adjustments) for the category of income checked above Part I (see instructions)	15	
16	Adjustments to line 15 (see instructions)	16	
17	Combine the amounts on lines 15 and 16. This is your net foreign source taxable income. (If the result is zero or less, you have no foreign tax credit for the category of income you checked above Part I. Skip lines 18 through 22. However, if you are filing more than one Form 1116, you must complete line 20.)	17	
18	**Individuals:** Enter the amount from Form 1040, line 41, or Form 1040NR, line 39. **Estates and trusts:** Enter your taxable income without the deduction for your exemption	18	
	Caution: *If you figured your tax using the lower rates on qualified dividends or capital gains, see instructions.*		
19	Divide line 17 by line 18. If line 17 is more than line 18, enter "1"		19
20	**Individuals:** Enter the amount from Form 1040, line 44. If you are a nonresident alien, enter the amount from Form 1040NR, line 42. **Estates and trusts:** Enter the amount from Form 1041, Schedule G, line 1a, or the total of Form 990-T, lines 36 and 37		20
	Caution: *If you are completing line 20 for separate category e (lump-sum distributions), see instructions.*		
21	Multiply line 20 by line 19 (maximum amount of credit)		21
22	Enter the **smaller** of line 14 or line 21. If this is the only Form 1116 you are filing, skip lines 23 through 27 and enter this amount on line 28. Otherwise, complete the appropriate line in Part IV (see instructions) ▶		22

Part IV Summary of Credits From Separate Parts III (see instructions)

23	Credit for taxes on passive category income	23	
24	Credit for taxes on general category income	24	
25	Credit for taxes on certain income re-sourced by treaty	25	
26	Credit for taxes on lump-sum distributions	26	
27	Add lines 23 through 26		27
28	Enter the **smaller** of line 20 or line 27		28
29	Reduction of credit for international boycott operations. See instructions for line 12		29
30	Subtract line 29 from line 28. This is your **foreign tax credit.** Enter here and on Form 1040, line 47; Form 1040NR, line 45; Form 1041, Schedule G, line 2a; or Form 990-T, line 40a ▶		30

Form **1116** (2012)

Form 2555- EZ

Form **2555-EZ**

Department of the Treasury
Internal Revenue Service (99)

Foreign Earned Income Exclusion

▶ Attach to Form 1040.
▶ **Information about Form 2555-EZ and its separate instructions is at *www.irs.gov/form2555*.**

OMB No. 1545-0074

20 12

Attachment
Sequence No. **34A**

Name shown on Form 1040

Your social security number

You May Use This Form If You:

- Are a U.S. citizen or a resident alien.
- Earned wages/salaries in a foreign country.
- Had total foreign earned income of $95,100 or less.
- Are filing a calendar year return that covers a 12-month period.

And You:

- Do not have self-employment income.
- Do not have business/moving expenses.
- Do not claim the foreign housing exclusion or deduction.

Part I Tests To See If You Can Take the Foreign Earned Income Exclusion

1 Bona Fide Residence Test

a Were you a bona fide resident of a foreign country or countries for a period that includes an entire tax year (see page 2 of the instructions)? . . . . ☐ **Yes** ☐ **No**
- If you answered "Yes," you meet this test. Fill in line 1b and then go to line 3.
- If you answered "No," you **do not** meet this test. Go to line 2 to see if you meet the Physical Presence Test.

b Enter the date your bona fide residence began ▶ _____, and ended (see instructions) ▶ _____ .

2 Physical Presence Test

a Were you physically present in a foreign country or countries for at least 330 full days during—
{ 2012 **or**
any other period of 12 months in a row starting or ending in 2012? } . . . . ☐ **Yes** ☐ **No**
- If you answered "Yes," you meet this test. Fill in line 2b and then go to line 3.
- If you answered "No," you **do not** meet this test. You **cannot** take the exclusion unless you meet the Bona Fide Residence Test above.

b The physical presence test is based on the 12-month period from ▶ _____ through ▶ _____ .

3 Tax Home Test. Was your tax home in a foreign country or countries throughout your period of bona fide residence or physical presence, whichever applies? . . . . ☐ **Yes** ☐ **No**
- If you answered "Yes," you can take the exclusion. Complete Part II below and then go to page 2.
- If you answered "No," you **cannot** take the exclusion. **Do not** file this form.

Part II General Information

4 Your foreign address (including country)	5 Your occupation

6 Employer's name	7 Employer's U.S. address (including ZIP code)	8 Employer's foreign address

9 Employer is (check any that apply):
a A U.S. business . . . . ☐
b A foreign business . . . . ☐
c Other (specify) ▶ _____ ☐
10a If you previously filed Form 2555 or 2555-EZ, enter the last year you filed the form. ▶ _____
b If you did not previously file Form 2555 or 2555-EZ, check here ▶ ☐ and go to line 11a now.
c Have you ever revoked the foreign earned income exclusion? . . . . ☐ **Yes** ☐**No**
d If you answered "Yes," enter the tax year for which the revocation was effective. ▶ _____
11a List your tax home(s) during 2012 and date(s) established. ▶ _____

b Of what country are you a citizen/national? ▶ _____

For Paperwork Reduction Act Notice, see the Form 1040 instructions.   Cat. No. 13272W   Form **2555-EZ** (2012)

Part III | **Days Present in the United States—** Complete this part if you were in the United States or its possessions during 2012.

12	(a) Date arrived in U.S.	(b) Date left U.S.	(c) Number of days in U.S. on business	(d) Income earned in U.S. on business (attach computation)

Part IV | **Figure Your Foreign Earned Income Exclusion**

13	Maximum foreign earned income exclusion	13	$95,100 00
14	Enter the number of days in your qualifying period that fall within 2012 .	14	days
15	Did you enter 366 on line 14? ☐ **Yes.** Enter "1.000." ☐ **No.** Divide line 14 by 366 and enter the result as a decimal (rounded to at least three places).	15	× .
16	Multiply line 13 by line 15	16	
17	Enter, in U.S. dollars, the total foreign earned income you earned and received in 2012 (see instructions). Be sure to include this amount on Form 1040, line 7	17	
18	**Foreign earned income exclusion.** Enter the **smaller** of line 16 or line 17 here and in parentheses on **Form 1040, line 21.** Next to the amount enter "2555-EZ." On Form 1040, subtract this amount from your income to arrive at total income on Form 1040, line 22 . . . . ▶	18	

Form **2555-EZ** (2012)

Form 2555

Form **2555** Department of the Treasury Internal Revenue Service	**Foreign Earned Income** ▶ Attach to Form 1040. ▶ Information about Form 2555 and its separate instructions is at *www.irs.gov/form2555*.	OMB No. 1545-0074 20**12** Attachment Sequence No. **34**

For Use by U.S. Citizens and Resident Aliens Only

Name shown on Form 1040	Your social security number

Part I — General Information

1 Your foreign address (including country)

2 Your occupation

3 Employer's name ▶

4a Employer's U.S. address ▶

b Employer's foreign address ▶

5 Employer is (check any that apply): ▶
- **a** ☐ A foreign entity
- **b** ☐ A U.S. company
- **c** ☐ Self
- **d** ☐ A foreign affiliate of a U.S. company
- **e** ☐ Other (specify) ▶

6a If you previously filed Form 2555 or Form 2555-EZ, enter the last year you filed the form. ▶

b If you did not previously file Form 2555 or 2555-EZ to claim either of the exclusions, check here ▶ ☐ and go to line 7.

c Have you ever revoked either of the exclusions? . . . . ☐ Yes ☐ No

d If you answered "Yes," enter the type of exclusion and the tax year for which the revocation was effective. ▶

7 Of what country are you a citizen/national? ▶

8a Did you maintain a separate foreign residence for your family because of adverse living conditions at your tax home? See **Second foreign household** in the instructions . . . . ☐ Yes ☐ No

b If "Yes," enter city and country of the separate foreign residence. Also, enter the number of days during your tax year that you maintained a second household at that address. ▶

9 List your tax home(s) during your tax year and date(s) established. ▶

Next, complete either Part II or Part III. If an item does not apply, enter "NA." If you do not give the information asked for, any exclusion or deduction you claim may be disallowed.

Part II — Taxpayers Qualifying Under Bona Fide Residence Test (see instructions)

10 Date bona fide residence began ▶ , and ended ▶

11 Kind of living quarters in foreign country ▶
- **a** ☐ Purchased house
- **b** ☐ Rented house or apartment
- **c** ☐ Rented room
- **d** ☐ Quarters furnished by employer

12a Did any of your family live with you abroad during any part of the tax year? . . . . ☐ Yes ☐ No

b If "Yes," who and for what period? ▶

13a Have you submitted a statement to the authorities of the foreign country where you claim bona fide residence that you are not a resident of that country? See instructions . . . . ☐ Yes ☐ No

b Are you required to pay income tax to the country where you claim bona fide residence? See instructions . ☐ Yes ☐ No

If you answered "Yes" to 13a and "No" to 13b, you do not qualify as a bona fide resident. Do not complete the rest of this part.

14 If you were present in the United States or its possessions during the tax year, complete columns **(a)–(d)** below. **Do not** include the income from column **(d)** in Part IV, but report it on Form 1040.

(a) Date arrived in U.S.	(b) Date left U.S.	(c) Number of days in U.S. on business	(d) Income earned in U.S. on business (attach computation)	(a) Date arrived in U.S.	(b) Date left U.S.	(c) Number of days in U.S. on business	(d) Income earned in U.S. on business (attach computation)

15a List any contractual terms or other conditions relating to the length of your employment abroad. ▶

b Enter the type of visa under which you entered the foreign country. ▶

c Did your visa limit the length of your stay or employment in a foreign country? If "Yes," attach explanation . ☐ Yes ☐ No

d Did you maintain a home in the United States while living abroad? . . . . ☐ Yes ☐ No

e If "Yes," enter address of your home, whether it was rented, the names of the occupants, and their relationship to you. ▶

For Paperwork Reduction Act Notice, see the Form 1040 instructions.　　　Cat. No. 11900P　　　Form **2555** (2012)

Part III Taxpayers Qualifying Under Physical Presence Test (see instructions)

16 The physical presence test is based on the 12-month period from ▶ _____ through ▶ _____

17 Enter your principal country of employment during your tax year. ▶ _____

18 If you traveled abroad during the 12-month period entered on line 16, complete columns **(a)–(f)** below. Exclude travel between foreign countries that did not involve travel on or over international waters, or in or over the United States, for 24 hours or more. If you have no travel to report during the period, enter "Physically present in a foreign country or countries for the entire 12-month period." **Do not** include the income from column **(f)** below in Part IV, but report it on Form 1040.

(a) Name of country (including U.S.)	**(b)** Date arrived	**(c)** Date left	**(d)** Full days present in country	**(e)** Number of days in U.S. on business	**(f)** Income earned in U.S. on business (attach computation)

Part IV All Taxpayers

Note: *Enter on lines 19 through 23 all income, including noncash income, you earned and actually or constructively received during your 2012 tax year for services you performed in a foreign country. If any of the foreign earned income received this tax year was earned in a prior tax year, or will be earned in a later tax year (such as a bonus), see the instructions.* **Do not** *include income from line 14, column* **(d)**, *or line 18, column* **(f)**. *Report amounts in U.S. dollars, using the exchange rates in effect when you actually or constructively received the income.*

If you are a cash basis taxpayer, report on Form 1040 all income you received in 2012, no matter when you performed the service.

2012 Foreign Earned Income		Amount (in U.S. dollars)	
19	Total wages, salaries, bonuses, commissions, etc.	**19**	
20	Allowable share of income for personal services performed (see instructions):		
a	In a business (including farming) or profession	**20a**	
b	In a partnership. List partnership's name and address and type of income. ▶ _____	**20b**	
21	Noncash income (market value of property or facilities furnished by employer—attach statement showing how it was determined):		
a	Home (lodging)	**21a**	
b	Meals	**21b**	
c	Car	**21c**	
d	Other property or facilities. List type and amount. ▶ _____	**21d**	
22	Allowances, reimbursements, or expenses paid on your behalf for services you performed:		
a	Cost of living and overseas differential **22a**		
b	Family **22b**		
c	Education **22c**		
d	Home leave **22d**		
e	Quarters **22e**		
f	For any other purpose. List type and amount. ▶ _____ **22f**		
g	Add lines 22a through 22f	**22g**	
23	Other foreign earned income. List type and amount. ▶ _____	**23**	
24	Add lines 19 through 21d, line 22g, and line 23	**24**	
25	Total amount of meals and lodging included on line 24 that is excludable (see instructions)	**25**	
26	Subtract line 25 from line 24. Enter the result here and on line 27 on page 3. This is your **2012 foreign earned income** ▶	**26**	

Form **2555** (2012)

Part V   All Taxpayers

27	Enter the amount from line 26	27	

Are you claiming the housing exclusion or housing deduction?
☐ **Yes.** Complete Part VI.
☐ **No.** Go to Part VII.

Part VI   Taxpayers Claiming the Housing Exclusion and/or Deduction

28	Qualified housing expenses for the tax year (see instructions)	28	
29a	Enter location where housing expenses incurred (see instructions) ▶ _____		
b	Enter limit on housing expenses (see instructions)	29b	
30	Enter the **smaller** of line 28 or line 29b	30	
31	Number of days in your qualifying period that fall within your 2012 tax year (see instructions) . . . . [31	] **days**		
32	Multiply $41.57 by the number of days on line 31. If 366 is entered on line 31, enter $15,216.00 here	32	
33	Subtract line 32 from line 30. If the result is zero or less, do not complete the rest of this part or any of Part IX	33	
34	Enter employer-provided amounts (see instructions) . . . . . [34	]		
35	Divide line 34 by line 27. Enter the result as a decimal (rounded to at least three places), but do not enter more than "1.000"	35	× .
36	**Housing exclusion.** Multiply line 33 by line 35. Enter the result but do not enter more than the amount on line 34. Also, complete Part VIII . . . . ▶	36	

Note: *The housing deduction is figured in Part IX. If you choose to claim the foreign earned income exclusion, complete Parts VII and VIII before Part IX.*

Part VII   Taxpayers Claiming the Foreign Earned Income Exclusion

37	Maximum foreign earned income exclusion	37	$95,100	00
38	• If you completed Part VI, enter the number from line 31.			
	• All others, enter the number of days in your qualifying period that fall within your 2012 tax year (see the instructions for line 31). } [38	] **days**			
39	• If line 38 and the number of days in your 2012 tax year (usually 366) are the same, enter "1.000."			
	• Otherwise, divide line 38 by the number of days in your 2012 tax year and enter the result as a decimal (rounded to at least three places). }	39	× .	
40	Multiply line 37 by line 39	40		
41	Subtract line 36 from line 27	41		
42	**Foreign earned income exclusion.** Enter the **smaller** of line 40 or line 41. Also, complete Part VIII ▶	42		

Part VIII   Taxpayers Claiming the Housing Exclusion, Foreign Earned Income Exclusion, or Both

43	Add lines 36 and 42	43	
44	Deductions allowed in figuring your adjusted gross income (Form 1040, line 37) that are allocable to the excluded income. See instructions and attach computation	44	
45	Subtract line 44 from line 43. Enter the result here and in parentheses on **Form 1040, line 21.** Next to the amount enter "Form 2555." On Form 1040, subtract this amount from your income to arrive at total income on Form 1040, line 22	45	

Part IX   Taxpayers Claiming the Housing Deduction—Complete this part only if **(a)** line 33 is more than line 36 and **(b)** line 27 is more than line 43.

46	Subtract line 36 from line 33	46	
47	Subtract line 43 from line 27	47	
48	Enter the **smaller** of line 46 or line 47	48	

Note: *If line 47 is **more than** line 48 and you could not deduct all of your 2011 housing deduction because of the 2011 limit, use the housing deduction carryover worksheet in the instructions to figure the amount to enter on line 49. Otherwise, go to line 50.*

49	Housing deduction carryover from 2011 (from housing deduction carryover worksheet in the instructions)	49	
50	**Housing deduction.** Add lines 48 and 49. Enter the total here and on Form 1040 to the left of line 36. Next to the amount on Form 1040, enter "Form 2555." Add it to the total adjustments reported on that line . . . . ▶	50	

Form **2555** (2012)

Form 3520

Form **3520**	**Annual Return To Report Transactions With Foreign Trusts and Receipt of Certain Foreign Gifts**	OMB No. 1545-0159
Department of the Treasury Internal Revenue Service	▶ Information about Form 3520 and its separate instructions is at *www.irs.gov/form3520*.	2012

Note. All information must be in English. Show all amounts in U.S. dollars. File a **separate** Form 3520 for **each** foreign trust.

For calendar year 2012, or tax year beginning _____ , 2012, ending _____ , 20 ___

A Check appropriate boxes: ☐ Initial return ☐ Final return ☐ Amended return

B Check box that applies to person filing return: ☐ Individual ☐ Partnership ☐ Corporation ☐ Trust ☐ Executor

Check all applicable boxes:

☐ **(a)** You are a U.S. transferor who, directly or indirectly, transferred money or other property during the current tax year to a foreign trust, **(b)** You held an outstanding obligation of a related foreign trust (or a person related to the trust) issued during the current tax year, that you reported as a "qualified obligation" (defined in the instructions) during the current tax year, or **(c)** You are the executor of the estate of a U.S. decedent and (1) the decedent made a transfer to a foreign trust by reason of death, (2) the decedent was treated as the owner of any portion of a foreign trust immediately prior to death, or (3) the decedent's estate included any portion of the assets of a foreign trust. **Complete all applicable identifying information requested below and Part I of the form** and see the instructions for Part I.

☐ You are a U.S. owner of all or any portion of a foreign trust at any time during the tax year. **Complete all applicable identifying information requested below and Part II of the form** and see the instructions for Part II.

☐ **(a)** You are a U.S. person who, during the current tax year, received a distribution from a foreign trust, or **(b)** You are a U.S. person who is also a grantor or beneficiary of a foreign trust (1) that has made a loan of cash or marketable securities, directly or indirectly, to you or a U.S. person related to you during the current tax year, or (2) from which you or a U.S. person related to you received the uncompensated use of trust property. **Complete all applicable identifying information requested below and Part III of the form** and see the instructions for Part III.

☐ You are a U.S. person who, during the current tax year, received certain gifts or bequests from a foreign person. **Complete all applicable identifying information requested below and Part IV of the form** and see the instructions for Part IV.

Service Center where U.S. person's income tax return is filed ▶ _____

1a Name of person(s) filing return (see instructions)		**b** Identification number
c Number, street, and room or suite no. (if a P.O. box, see instructions)		**d** Spouse's identification number
e City or town	**f** State or province	**g** ZIP or postal code	**h** Country
2a Name of foreign trust (if applicable)		**b** Employer identification number (if any)
c Number, street, and room or suite no. (if a P.O. box, see instructions)		
d City or town	**e** State or province	**f** ZIP or postal code	**g** Country

3 Did the foreign trust appoint a U.S. agent (defined in the instructions) who can provide the IRS with all relevant trust information? . . . . ☐ Yes ☐ No

If "Yes," complete lines 3a through 3g. If "No," be sure to complete Part I, lines 15 through 18.

3a Name of U.S. agent		**b** Identification number (if any)
c Number, street, and room or suite no. (if a P.O. box, see instructions)		
d City or town	**e** State or province	**f** ZIP or postal code	**g** Country
4a Name of U.S. decedent (see instr.)	**b** Address	**c** TIN of decedent
d Date of death		**e** EIN of estate

f Check applicable box:

☐ U.S. decedent made transfer to a foreign trust by reason of death.

☐ U.S. decedent treated as owner of foreign trust immediately prior to death.

☐ Assets of foreign trust were included in estate of U.S. decedent.

Sign Here

Under penalties of perjury, I declare that I have examined this return, including any accompanying reports, schedules, or statements, and to the best of my knowledge and belief, it is true, correct, and complete.

▶ Signature _____ ▶ Title _____ ▶ Date _____

Paid Preparer Use Only

Print/Type preparer's name	Preparer's signature	Date	Check ☐ if self-employed	PTIN
Firm's name ▶			Firm's EIN ▶	
Firm's address ▶			Phone no.	

For Privacy Act and Paperwork Reduction Act Notice, see instructions.   Cat. No. 19594V   Form **3520** (2012)

Part I	**Transfers by U.S. Persons to a Foreign Trust During the Current Tax Year** (see instructions)

5a Name of trust creator | **b** Address | **c** Identification number (if any)

6a Country code of country where trust was created | **b** Country code of country whose law governs the trust | **c** Date trust was created

7a Will any person (other than the U.S. transferor or the foreign trust) be treated as the owner of the transferred assets after the transfer? ☐ **Yes** ☐ **No**

b

(i) Name of other foreign trust owners, if any	(ii) Address	(iii) Country of residence	(iv) Identification number, if any	(v) Relevant Code section

8 Was the transfer a completed gift or bequest? If "Yes," see instructions . . . . ☐ **Yes** ☐ **No**

9a Now or in the future, can any part of the income or corpus of the trust benefit any U.S. beneficiary? . . . . . ☐ **Yes** ☐ **No**

b If "No," could the trust be revised or amended to benefit a U.S. beneficiary? . . . . ☐ **Yes** ☐ **No**

10 Will you continue to be treated as the owner of the transferred asset(s) after the transfer? . . . . ☐ **Yes** ☐ **No**

Schedule A—Obligations of a Related Trust (see instructions)

11a During the current tax year, did you transfer property (including cash) to a related foreign trust in exchange for an obligation of the trust or an obligation of a person related to the trust (see instructions)? . . . . ☐ **Yes** ☐ **No**

If "Yes," complete the rest of Schedule A, as applicable. If "No," go to Schedule B.

b Were any of the obligations you received (with respect to a transfer described in 11a above) qualified obligations? . ☐ **Yes** ☐ **No**

If "Yes," complete the rest of Schedule A with respect to each qualified obligation.

If "No," go to Schedule B and, when completing columns (a) through (i) of line 13 with respect to each nonqualified obligation, enter "-0-" in column (h).

(i) Date of transfer giving rise to obligation	(ii) Maximum term	(iii) Yield to maturity	(iv) FMV of obligation

12 With respect to each qualified obligation you reported on line 11b: Do you agree to extend the period of assessment of any income or transfer tax attributable to the transfer, and any consequential income tax changes for each year that the obligation is outstanding, to a date 3 years after the maturity date of the obligation? . . . . ☐ **Yes** ☐ **No**

Note. Generally, you must answer "Yes," if you checked "Yes" to the question on line 11b.

Schedule B—Gratuitous Transfers (see instructions)

13 During the current tax year, did you make any transfers (directly or indirectly) to the trust and receive less than FMV, or no consideration at all, for the property transferred? . . . . ☐ **Yes** ☐ **No**

If "Yes," complete columns (a) through (i) below and the rest of Schedule B, as applicable.

If "No," go to Schedule C.

(a) Date of transfer	(b) Description of property transferred	(c) FMV of property transferred	(d) U.S. adjusted basis of property transferred	(e) Gain recognized at time of transfer, if any	(f) Excess, if any, of column (c) over the sum of columns (d) and (e)	(g) Description of property received, if any	(h) FMV of property received	(i) Excess of column (c) over column (h)
Totals ▶					$		$	

14 You are required to attach a copy of each sale or loan document entered into in connection with a transfer reported on line 13. If these documents have been attached to a Form 3520 filed within the previous 3 years, attach only relevant updates.

Are you attaching a copy of:	Yes	No	Attached Previously	Year Attached
a Sale document?	☐	☐	☐	_____
b Loan document?	☐	☐	☐	_____
c Subsequent variances to original sale or loan documents?	☐	☐	☐	_____

Form **3520** (2012)

Part I	**Schedule B—Gratuitous Transfers** *(Continued)*

Note. Complete lines 15 through 18 only if you answered "No" to line 3, acknowledging that the foreign trust did not appoint a U.S. agent to provide the IRS with all relevant trust information.

15	(a) Name of beneficiary	(b) Address of beneficiary	(c) U.S. beneficiary?		(d) Identification number, if any
			Yes	**No**	

16	(a) Name of trustee	(b) Address of trustee	(c) Identification number, if any

17	(a) Name of other persons with trust powers	(b) Address of other persons with trust powers	(c) Description of powers	(d) Identification number, if any

18   If you checked "No" on line 3 (or did not complete lines 3a through 3g), you are required to attach a copy of all trust documents as indicated below. If these documents have been attached to a Form 3520-A filed within the previous 3 years, attach only relevant updates.

	Are you attaching a copy of:	Yes	No	Attached Previously	Year Attached
a	Summary of all written and oral agreements and understandings relating to the trust?	☐	☐	☐	_____
b	The trust instrument?	☐	☐	☐	_____
c	Memoranda or letters of wishes?	☐	☐	☐	_____
d	Subsequent variances to original trust documents?	☐	☐	☐	_____
e	Trust financial statements?	☐	☐	☐	_____
f	Other trust documents?	☐	☐	☐	_____

Schedule C—Qualified Obligations Outstanding in the Current Tax Year (see instructions)

19   Did you, at any time during the tax year, hold an outstanding obligation of a related foreign trust (or a person related to the trust) that you reported as a "qualified obligation" in the current tax year? . . . . ☐ **Yes**   ☐ **No**

If "Yes," complete columns (a) through (e) below.

(a) Date of original obligation	(b) Tax year qualified obligation first reported	(c) Amount of principal payments made during the tax year	(d) Amount of interest payments made during the tax year	(e) Does the obligation still meet the criteria for a qualified obligation?	
				Yes	No

Part II	U.S. Owner of a Foreign Trust (see instructions)

20	(a) Name of other foreign trust owners, if any	(b) Address	(c) Country of residence	(d) Identification number, if any	(e) Relevant Code section

21	(a) Country code of country where foreign trust was created	(b) Country code of country whose law governs the foreign trust	(c) Date foreign trust was created

22 Did the foreign trust file Form 3520-A for the current year? . . . . ☐ Yes ☐ No

If "Yes," attach the Foreign Grantor Trust Owner Statement you received from the foreign trust.

If "No," to the best of your ability, complete and attach a substitute Form 3520-A for the foreign trust.

See instructions for information on penalties.

23 Enter the gross value of the portion of the foreign trust that you are treated as owning . . . . ▶ $

Part III	Distributions to a U.S. Person From a Foreign Trust During the Current Tax Year (see instructions)

24 Cash amounts or FMV of property received, directly or indirectly, during the current tax year, from the foreign trust (exclude loans included on line 25).

(a) Date of distribution	(b) Description of property received	(c) FMV of property received (determined on date of distribution)	(d) Description of property transferred, if any	(e) FMV of property transferred	(f) Excess of column (c) over column (e)

Totals. . . . . ▶ $

25 During the current tax year, did you (or a person related to you) receive a loan from a related foreign trust (including an extension of credit upon the purchase of property from the trust)? . . . . ☐ Yes ☐ No

If "Yes," complete columns (a) through (g) below for each such loan.

Note. You are considered to have received a loan if you (or a U.S. person related to you) were permitted the uncompensated use of trust property (as described in section 643(i)). See instructions for additional information, including how to complete columns (a) through (g) for such transactions.

(a) FMV of loan proceeds	(b) Date of original loan transaction	(c) Maximum term of repayment of obligation	(d) Interest rate of obligation	(e) Is the obligation a "qualified obligation?"		(f) FMV of qualified obligation	(g) Amount treated as distribution from the trust (subtract column (f) from column (a))
				Yes	No		

Total . . . . ▶ $

26 With respect to each obligation you reported as a "qualified obligation" on line 25: Do you agree to extend the period of assessment of any income or transfer tax attributable to the transaction, and any consequential income tax changes for each year that the obligation is outstanding, to a date 3 years after the maturity date of the obligation? . . . . ☐ Yes ☐ No

Note. Generally, you must answer "Yes" if you checked "Yes" in column (e) of line 25.

27 Total distributions received during the current tax year. Add line 24, column (f), and line 25, column (g) . . ▶ $

28 Did the trust, at any time during the tax year, hold an outstanding obligation of yours (or a person related to you) that you reported as a "qualified obligation" in the current tax year? . . . . ☐ Yes ☐ No

If "Yes," complete columns (a) through (e) below for each obligation.

(a) Date of original loan transaction	(b) Tax year qualified obligation first reported	(c) Amount of principal payments made during the tax year	(d) Amount of interest payments made during the tax year	(e) Does the loan still meet the criteria of a qualified obligation?	
				Yes	No

Form **3520** (2012)

Part III	Distributions to a U.S. Person From a Foreign Trust During the Current Tax Year *(Continued)*

29 Did you receive a Foreign Grantor Trust Beneficiary Statement from the foreign trust with respect to a distribution? . . . . ☐ Yes ☐ No ☐ N/A

If "Yes," attach the statement and do not complete the remainder of Part III with respect to that distribution.
If "No," complete Schedule A with respect to that distribution. Also complete Schedule C if you enter an amount greater than zero on line 37.

30 Did you receive a Foreign Nongrantor Trust Beneficiary Statement from the foreign trust with respect to a distribution? . . . . ☐ Yes ☐ No ☐ N/A

If "Yes," attach the statement and complete either Schedule A or Schedule B below (see instructions). Also complete Schedule C if you enter an amount greater than zero on line 37 or line 41a.

If "No," complete Schedule A with respect to that distribution. Also complete Schedule C if you enter an amount greater than zero on line 37.

Schedule A—Default Calculation of Trust Distributions (see instructions)

31	Enter amount from line 27	
32	Number of years the trust has been a foreign trust (see instructions) . . . . . ▶	
33	Enter total distributions received from the foreign trust during the 3 preceding tax years (or during the number of years the trust has been a foreign trust, if fewer than 3)	
34	Multiply line 33 by 1.25	
35	Average distribution. Divide line 34 by 3 (or the number of years the trust has been a foreign trust, if fewer than 3) and enter the result	
36	Amount treated as ordinary income earned in the current year. Enter the smaller of line 31 or line 35.	
37	Amount treated as accumulation distribution. Subtract line 36 from line 31. If -0-, do not complete the rest of Part III	
38	Applicable number of years of trust. Divide line 32 by 2 and enter the result here . ▶	

Schedule B—Actual Calculation of Trust Distributions (see instructions)

39	Enter amount from line 27	
40a	Amount treated as ordinary income in the current tax year	
b	Qualified dividends . . . . ▶	
41a	Amount treated as accumulation distribution. If -0-, do not complete Schedule C, Part III	
b	Amount of line 41a that is tax-exempt . . . . ▶	
42a	Amount treated as net short-term capital gain in the current tax year	
b	Amount treated as net long-term capital gain in the current tax year	
c	28% rate gain . . . . ▶	
d	Unrecaptured section 1250 gain . . . . ▶	
43	Amount treated as distribution from trust corpus	
44	Enter any other distributed amount received from the foreign trust not included on lines 40a, 41a, 42a, 42b, and 43 (attach explanation)	
45	Amount of foreign trust's aggregate undistributed net income	
46	Amount of foreign trust's weighted undistributed net income	
47	Applicable number of years of trust. Divide line 46 by line 45 and enter the result here ▶	

Schedule C—Calculation of Interest Charge (see instructions)

48	Enter accumulation distribution from line 37 or 41a, as applicable	
49	Enter tax on total accumulation distribution from line 28 of Form 4970 (attach Form 4970—see instructions) . .	
50	Enter applicable number of years of foreign trust from line 38 or 47, as applicable (round to nearest half-year) . . . . ▶	
51	Combined interest rate imposed on the total accumulation distribution (see instructions)	
52	Interest charge. Multiply the amount on line 49 by the combined interest rate on line 51	
53	Tax attributable to accumulation distributions. Add lines 49 and 52. Enter here and as "additional tax" on your income tax return	

Form **3520** (2012)

Part IV U.S. Recipients of Gifts or Bequests Received During the Current Tax Year From Foreign Persons
(see instructions)

54 During the current tax year, did you receive more than $100,000 that you treated as gifts or bequests from a nonresident alien or a foreign estate? See instructions for special rules regarding related donors . . . . . . ☐ **Yes** ☐ **No**

If "Yes," complete columns (a) through (c) with respect to each such gift or bequest in excess of $5,000. If more space is needed, attach a statement.

(a) Date of gift or bequest	(b) Description of property received	(c) FMV of property received

Total . . . . ▶	$

55 During the current tax year, did you receive more than $14,723 that you treated as gifts from a foreign corporation or a foreign partnership? See instructions regarding related donors. . . . . ☐ **Yes** ☐ **No**

If "Yes," complete columns (a) through (g) with respect to each such gift. If more space is needed, attach a statement.

(a) Date of gift	(b) Name of foreign donor	(c) Address of foreign donor	(d) Identification number, if any

(e) Check the box that applies to the foreign donor		(f) Description of property received	(g) FMV of property received
Corporation	Partnership		

56 Do you have any reason to believe that the foreign donor, in making any gift or bequest described in lines 54 and 55, was acting as a nominee or intermediary for any other person? If "Yes," see instructions . . . . ☐ **Yes** ☐ **No**

Form **3520** (2012)

Form 5471

(Rev. December 2012)

Department of the Treasury
Internal Revenue Service

Information Return of U.S. Persons With Respect To Certain Foreign Corporations

► For more information about Form 5471, see www.irs.gov/form5471

Information furnished for the foreign corporation's annual accounting period (tax year required by section 898) (see instructions) beginning   , 20   , and ending   , 20

OMB No. 1545-0704

Attachment Sequence No. **121**

Name of person filing this return	A Identifying number

Number, street, and room or suite no. (or P.O. box number if mail is not delivered to street address)	B Category of filer (See instructions. Check applicable box(es)): 1 (repealed) 2 ☐ 3 ☐ 4 ☐ 5 ☐

City or town, state, and ZIP code	C Enter the total percentage of the foreign corporation's voting stock you owned at the end of its annual accounting period %

Filer's tax year beginning   , 20   , and ending   , 20

D Person(s) on whose behalf this information return is filed:

(1) Name	(2) Address	(3) Identifying number	(4) Check applicable box(es)		
			Shareholder	Officer	Director

Important: *Fill in all applicable lines and schedules. All information* **must** *be in English. All amounts* **must** *be stated in U.S. dollars unless otherwise indicated.*

1a Name and address of foreign corporation	b(1) Employer identification number, if any
	b(2) Reference ID number (see instructions)
	c Country under whose laws incorporated

d Date of incorporation	e Principal place of business	f Principal business activity code number	g Principal business activity	h Functional currency

2 Provide the following information for the foreign corporation's accounting period stated above.

a Name, address, and identifying number of branch office or agent (if any) in the United States	b If a U.S. income tax return was filed, enter:	
	(i) Taxable income or (loss)	(ii) U.S. income tax paid (after all credits)

c Name and address of foreign corporation's statutory or resident agent in country of incorporation	d Name and address (including corporate department, if applicable) of person (or persons) with custody of the books and records of the foreign corporation, and the location of such books and records, if different

Schedule A Stock of the Foreign Corporation

(a) Description of each class of stock	(b) Number of shares issued and outstanding	
	(i) Beginning of annual accounting period	(ii) End of annual accounting period

For Paperwork Reduction Act Notice, see instructions.   Cat. No. 49958V   Form **5471** (Rev. 12-2012)

Schedule B   U.S. Shareholders of Foreign Corporation (see instructions)

(a) Name, address, and identifying number of shareholder	(b) Description of each class of stock held by shareholder. **Note:** *This description should match the corresponding description entered in Schedule A, column (a).*	(c) Number of shares held at beginning of annual accounting period	(d) Number of shares held at end of annual accounting period	(e) Pro rata share of subpart F income (enter as a percentage)

Schedule C   Income Statement (see instructions)

Important: *Report all information in functional currency in accordance with U.S. GAAP. Also, report each amount in U.S. dollars translated from functional currency (using GAAP translation rules). However, if the functional currency is the U.S. dollar, complete only the U.S. Dollars column. See instructions for special rules for DASTM corporations.*

				Functional Currency	U.S. Dollars
Income	1a	Gross receipts or sales	1a		
	b	Returns and allowances	1b		
	c	Subtract line 1b from line 1a	1c		
	2	Cost of goods sold	2		
	3	Gross profit (subtract line 2 from line 1c)	3		
	4	Dividends	4		
	5	Interest	5		
	6a	Gross rents	6a		
	b	Gross royalties and license fees	6b		
	7	Net gain or (loss) on sale of capital assets	7		
	8	Other income (attach statement)	8		
	9	Total income (add lines 3 through 8)	9		
Deductions	10	Compensation not deducted elsewhere	10		
	11a	Rents	11a		
	b	Royalties and license fees	11b		
	12	Interest	12		
	13	Depreciation not deducted elsewhere	13		
	14	Depletion	14		
	15	Taxes (exclude provision for income, war profits, and excess profits taxes)	15		
	16	Other deductions (attach statement—exclude provision for income, war profits, and excess profits taxes)	16		
	17	Total deductions (add lines 10 through 16)	17		
Net Income	18	Net income or (loss) before extraordinary items, prior period adjustments, and the provision for income, war profits, and excess profits taxes (subtract line 17 from line 9)	18		
	19	Extraordinary items and prior period adjustments (see instructions)	19		
	20	Provision for income, war profits, and excess profits taxes (see instructions)	20		
	21	Current year net income or (loss) per books (combine lines 18 through 20)	21		

Form **5471** (Rev. 12-2012)

Schedule E Income, War Profits, and Excess Profits Taxes Paid or Accrued (see instructions)

(a) Name of country or U.S. possession	Amount of tax		
	(b) In foreign currency	**(c)** Conversion rate	**(d)** In U.S. dollars
1 U.S.			
2			
3			
4			
5			
6			
7			
8 Total . . . . ▶			

Schedule F Balance Sheet

Important: *Report all amounts in U.S. dollars prepared and translated in accordance with U.S. GAAP. See instructions for an exception for DASTM corporations.*

Assets		(a) Beginning of annual accounting period	(b) End of annual accounting period
1 Cash	1		
2a Trade notes and accounts receivable	2a		
b Less allowance for bad debts	2b	(	)( )
3 Inventories	3		
4 Other current assets (attach statement)	4		
5 Loans to shareholders and other related persons	5		
6 Investment in subsidiaries (attach statement)	6		
7 Other investments (attach statement)	7		
8a Buildings and other depreciable assets	8a		
b Less accumulated depreciation	8b	(	)( )
9a Depletable assets	9a		
b Less accumulated depletion	9b	(	)( )
10 Land (net of any amortization)	10		
11 Intangible assets:			
a Goodwill	11a		
b Organization costs	11b		
c Patents, trademarks, and other intangible assets	11c		
d Less accumulated amortization for lines 11a, b, and c	11d	(	)( )
12 Other assets (attach statement)	12		
13 Total assets	13		

Liabilities and Shareholders' Equity			
14 Accounts payable	14		
15 Other current liabilities (attach statement)	15		
16 Loans from shareholders and other related persons	16		
17 Other liabilities (attach statement)	17		
18 Capital stock:			
a Preferred stock	18a		
b Common stock	18b		
19 Paid-in or capital surplus (attach reconciliation)	19		
20 Retained earnings	20		
21 Less cost of treasury stock	21	(	)( )
22 Total liabilities and shareholders' equity	22		

Form **5471** (Rev. 12-2012)

Schedule G   Other Information

		Yes	No
1	During the tax year, did the foreign corporation own at least a 10% interest, directly or indirectly, in any foreign partnership?	☐	☐
	If "Yes," see the instructions for required statement.		
2	During the tax year, did the foreign corporation own an interest in any trust?	☐	☐
3	During the tax year, did the foreign corporation own any foreign entities that were disregarded as entities separate from their owners under Regulations sections 301.7701-2 and 301.7701-3 (see instructions)?	☐	☐
	If "Yes," you are generally required to attach Form 8858 for each entity (see instructions).		
4	During the tax year, was the foreign corporation a participant in any cost sharing arrangement?	☐	☐
5	During the course of the tax year, did the foreign corporation become a participant in any cost sharing arrangement?	☐	☐
6	During the tax year, did the foreign corporation participate in any reportable transaction as defined in Regulations section 1.6011-4?	☐	☐
	If "Yes," attach Form(s) 8886 if required by Regulations section 1.6011-4(c)(3)(i)(G).		
7	During the tax year, did the foreign corporation pay or accrue any foreign tax that was disqualified for credit under section 901(m)?	☐	☐
8	During the tax year, did the foreign corporation pay or accrue foreign taxes to which section 909 applies, or treat foreign taxes that were previously suspended under section 909 as no longer suspended?	☐	☐

Schedule H   Current Earnings and Profits (see instructions)

Important: *Enter the amounts on lines 1 through 5c in **functional** currency.*

		Net Additions	Net Subtractions	
1	Current year net income or (loss) per foreign books of account			**1**
2	Net adjustments made to line 1 to determine current earnings and profits according to U.S. financial and tax accounting standards (see instructions):			
a	Capital gains or losses			
b	Depreciation and amortization			
c	Depletion			
d	Investment or incentive allowance			
e	Charges to statutory reserves			
f	Inventory adjustments			
g	Taxes			
h	Other (attach statement)			
3	Total net additions			
4	Total net subtractions			
5a	Current earnings and profits (line 1 plus line 3 minus line 4)			**5a**
b	DASTM gain or (loss) for foreign corporations that use DASTM (see instructions)			**5b**
c	Combine lines 5a and 5b			**5c**
d	Current earnings and profits in U.S. dollars (line 5c translated at the appropriate exchange rate as defined in section 989(b) and the related regulations (see instructions))			**5d**
	Enter exchange rate used for line 5d ▶			

Schedule I   Summary of Shareholder's Income From Foreign Corporation (see instructions)

If item D on page 1 is completed, a separate Schedule I must be filed for each Category 4 or 5 filer for whom reporting is furnished on this Form 5471. This schedule I is being completed for:

Name of U.S. shareholder ▶   Identifying number ▶

1	Subpart F income (line 38b, Worksheet A in the instructions)	**1**	
2	Earnings invested in U.S. property (line 17, Worksheet B in the instructions)	**2**	
3	Previously excluded subpart F income withdrawn from qualified investments (line 6b, Worksheet C in the instructions)	**3**	
4	Previously excluded export trade income withdrawn from investment in export trade assets (line 7b, Worksheet D in the instructions)	**4**	
5	Factoring income	**5**	
6	Total of lines 1 through 5. Enter here and on your income tax return. See instructions	**6**	
7	Dividends received (translated at spot rate on payment date under section 989(b)(1))	**7**	
8	Exchange gain or (loss) on a distribution of previously taxed income	**8**	

	Yes	No
• Was any income of the foreign corporation blocked?	☐	☐
• Did any such income become unblocked during the tax year (see section 964(b))?	☐	☐
If the answer to either question is "Yes," attach an explanation.		

Form 8621

Form 8621 (Rev. December 2011) Department of the Treasury Internal Revenue Service	**Information Return by a Shareholder of a Passive Foreign Investment Company or Qualified Electing Fund** ▶ See separate instructions.	OMB No. 1545-1002 Attachment Sequence No. **69**

Name of shareholder	Identifying number (see instructions)

Number, street, and room or suite no. (If a P.O. box, see instructions.)	Shareholder tax year: calendar year 20_____ or other tax year beginning _____ , 20 ____ and ending _____ , 20 ____

City or town, state, and ZIP code or country

Check type of shareholder filing the return: ☐ Individual ☐ Corporation ☐ Partnership ☐ S Corporation ☐ Nongrantor Trust ☐ Estate

Name of passive foreign investment company (PFIC) or qualified electing fund (QEF)	Employer identification number (if any)

Address (Enter number, street, city or town, and country.)	Tax year of company or fund: calendar year 20_____ or other tax year beginning _____ , 20 ____ and ending _____ , 20 ____ .

Part I   Elections (See instructions.)

A ☐ **Election To Treat the PFIC as a QEF.** I, a shareholder of a PFIC, elect to treat the PFIC as a QEF. *Complete lines 1a through 2c of Part II.*

B ☐ **Deemed Sale Election.** I, a shareholder on the first day of a PFIC's first tax year as a QEF, elect to recognize gain on the deemed sale of my interest in the PFIC. *Enter gain or loss on line 10f of Part IV.*

C ☐ **Deemed Dividend Election.** I, a shareholder on the first day of a PFIC's first tax year as a QEF that is a controlled foreign corporation (CFC), elect to treat an amount equal to my share of the post-1986 earnings and profits of the CFC as an excess distribution. *Enter this amount on line 10e of Part IV.*

D ☐ **Election To Extend Time For Payment of Tax.** I, a shareholder of a QEF, elect to extend the time for payment of tax on the undistributed earnings and profits of the QEF until this election is terminated. *Complete lines 3a through 4c of Part II to calculate the tax that may be deferred.*

Note: *If any portion of line 1a or line 2a of Part II is includible under section 951, you may **not** make this election. Also, see sections 1294(c) and 1294(f) and the related regulations for events that terminate this election.*

E ☐ **Election To Recognize Gain on Deemed Sale of PFIC.** I, a shareholder of a former PFIC or a PFIC to which section 1297(d) applies, elect to treat as an excess distribution the gain recognized on the deemed sale of my interest in the PFIC, or, if I qualify, my share of the PFIC's post-1986 earnings and profits deemed distributed, on the last day of its last tax year as a PFIC under section 1297(a). *Enter gain on line 10f of Part IV.*

F ☐ **Election To Mark-to-Market PFIC Stock.** I, a shareholder of a PFIC, elect to mark-to-market the PFIC stock that is marketable within the meaning of section 1296(e). *Complete Part III.*

G ☐ **Deemed Dividend Election With Respect to a Section 1297(e) PFIC.** I, a shareholder of a section 1297(e) PFIC, within the meaning of Regulations section 1.1291-9(j)(2)(v), elect to make a deemed dividend election with respect to the Section 1297(e) PFIC. My holding period in the stock of the Section 1297(e) PFIC includes the CFC qualification date, as defined in Regulations section 1.1297-3(d).

H ☐ **Deemed Dividend Election With Respect to a Former PFIC.** I, a shareholder of a former PFIC, within the meaning of Regulations section 1.1291-9(j)(2)(iv), elect to make a deemed dividend election with respect to the former PFIC. My holding period in the stock of the former PFIC includes the termination date, as defined in Regulations section 1.1298-3(d).

Part II   Income From a Qualified Electing Fund (QEF). All QEF shareholders complete lines 1a through 2c. If you are making Election D, also complete lines 3a through 4c. (See instructions.)

1a	Enter your pro rata share of the ordinary earnings of the QEF	**1a**	
b	Enter the portion of line 1a that is included in income under section 951 or that may be excluded under section 1293(g)	**1b**	
c	Subtract line 1b from line 1a. Enter this amount on your tax return as ordinary income		**1c**
2a	Enter your pro rata share of the total net capital gain of the QEF	**2a**	
b	Enter the portion of line 2a that is included in income under section 951 or that may be excluded under section 1293(g)	**2b**	
c	Subtract line 2b from line 2a. This amount is a net long-term capital gain. Enter this amount in Part II of the Schedule D used for your income tax return. (See instructions.)		**2c**
3a	Add lines 1c and 2c		**3a**
b	Enter the total amount of cash and the fair market value of other property distributed or deemed distributed to you during the tax year of the QEF. (See instructions.)	**3b**	
c	Enter the portion of line 3a not already included in line 3b that is attributable to shares in the QEF that you disposed of, pledged, or otherwise transferred during the tax year	**3c**	
d	Add lines 3b and 3c		**3d**
e	Subtract line 3d from line 3a, and enter the difference (if zero or less, enter amount in brackets)		**3e**
	Important: *If line 3e is greater than zero, and no portion of line 1a or 2a is includible in income under section 951, you may make Election D with respect to the amount on line 3e.*		
4a	Enter the total tax for the tax year (See instructions.)	**4a**	
b	Enter the total tax for the tax year determined without regard to the amount entered on line 3e	**4b**	
c	Subtract line 4b from line 4a. **This is the deferred tax, the time for payment of which is extended by making Election D. See instructions**		**4c**

For Disclosure, Privacy Act, and Paperwork Reduction Act Notice, see separate instructions.   Cat. No. 64174H   Form **8621** (Rev. 12-2011)

Part III	Gain or (Loss) From Mark-to-Market Election (See instructions.)		
5a	Enter the fair market value of your PFIC stock at the end of the tax year	5a	
b	Enter your adjusted basis in the stock at the end of the tax year	5b	
c	Subtract line 5b from line 5a. If a gain, do not complete lines 6 and 7. Include this amount as ordinary income on your tax return. If a loss, go to line 6	5c	
6	Enter any unreversed inclusions (as defined in section 1296(d))	6	
7	Enter the loss from line 5c, but only to the extent of unreversed inclusions on line 6. Include this amount as an ordinary loss on your tax return	7	
8	**If you sold or otherwise disposed of any section 1296 stock (see instructions) during the tax year:**		
a	Enter the fair market value of the stock on the date of sale or disposition	8a	
b	Enter the adjusted basis of the stock on the date of sale or disposition	8b	
c	Subtract line 8b from line 8a. If a gain, do not complete line 9. Include this amount as ordinary income on your tax return. If a loss, go to line 9	8c	
9a	Enter any unreversed inclusions (as defined in section 1296(d))	9a	
b	Enter the loss from line 8c, but only to the extent of unreversed inclusions on line 9a. Include this amount as an ordinary loss on your tax return. If the loss on line 8c exceeds unreversed inclusions on line 9a, complete line 9c	9b	
c	Enter the amount by which the loss on line 8c exceeds unreversed inclusions on line 9a. Include this amount on your tax return according to the rules generally applicable for losses provided elsewhere in the Code and regulations	9c	
	Note. See instructions in case of multiple dispositions.		

Part IV	Distributions From and Dispositions of Stock of a Section 1291 Fund (See instructions.) *Complete a **separate** Part IV for each excess distribution (see instructions).*		
10a	Enter your total distributions from the section 1291 fund during the current tax year with respect to the applicable stock. If the holding period of the stock began in the current tax year, see instructions	10a	
b	Enter the total distributions (reduced by the portions of such distributions that were excess distributions but not included in income under section 1291(a)(1)(B)) made by the fund with respect to the applicable stock for each of the 3 years preceding the current tax year (or if shorter, the portion of the shareholder's holding period before the current tax year)	10b	
c	Divide line 10b by 3. (See instructions if the number of preceding tax years is less than 3.)	10c	
d	Multiply line 10c by 125% (1.25)	10d	
e	Subtract line 10d from line 10a. This amount, if more than zero, is the excess distribution with respect to the applicable stock. If zero or less and you did not dispose of stock during the tax year, **do not** complete the rest of Part IV. See instructions if you received more than one distribution during the current tax year. Also, see instructions for rules for reporting a nonexcess distribution on your income tax return	10e	
f	Enter gain or loss from the disposition of stock of a section 1291 fund or former section 1291 fund. If a gain, complete line 11. If a loss, show it in brackets and **do not** complete line 11.	10f	
11a	Attach a statement for each distribution and disposition. Show your holding period for each share of stock or block of shares held. Allocate the excess distribution to each day in your holding period. Add all amounts that are allocated to days in each tax year.		
b	Enter the total of the amounts determined in line 11a that are allocable to the current tax year and tax years before the foreign corporation became a PFIC (pre-PFIC tax years). Enter these amounts on your income tax return as other income	11b	
c	Enter the aggregate increases in tax (before credits) for each tax year in your holding period (other than the current tax year and pre-PFIC years). (See instructions.)	11c	
d	Foreign tax credit. (See instructions.)	11d	
e	Subtract line 11d from line 11c. Enter this amount on your income tax return as "additional tax." (See instructions.)	11e	
f	Determine interest on each net increase in tax determined on line 11e using the rates and methods of section 6621. Enter the aggregate amount of interest here. (See instructions.)	11f	

Form **8621** (Rev. 12-2011)

Part V   Status of Prior Year Section 1294 Elections and Termination of Section 1294 Elections

Complete a separate column for each outstanding election. Complete lines 9 and 10 only if there is a partial termination of the section 1294 election.

		(i)	(ii)	(iii)	(iv)	(v)	(vi)
1	Tax year of outstanding election						
2	Undistributed earnings to which the election relates .						
3	Deferred tax						
4	Interest accrued on deferred tax (line 3) as of the filing date						
5	Event terminating election .						
6	Earnings distributed or deemed distributed during the tax year						
7	Deferred tax due with this return						
8	Accrued interest due with this return						
9	Deferred tax outstanding after partial termination of election .						
10	Interest accrued after partial termination of election . .						

Form **8621** (Rev. 12-2011)

Form 8865

Form **8865**	**Return of U.S. Persons With Respect to Certain Foreign Partnerships** ► Attach to your tax return. ► **Information about Form 8865 and its separate instructions is at** *www.irs.gov/form8865.*	OMB No. 1545-1668 **2012**
Department of the Treasury Internal Revenue Service	Information furnished for the foreign partnership's tax year beginning , 2012, and ending , 20	Attachment Sequence No. **118**

Name of person filing this return		Filer's identifying number

Filer's address (if you are not filing this form with your tax return)	**A** Category of filer (see **Categories of Filers** in the instructions and check applicable box(es)): 1 ☐ 2 ☐ 3 ☐ 4 ☐
	B Filer's tax year beginning , 20 , and ending , 20

C Filer's share of liabilities: Nonrecourse $ Qualified nonrecourse financing $ Other $

D If filer is a member of a consolidated group but not the parent, enter the following information about the parent:

Name EIN

Address

E Information about certain other partners (see instructions)

(1) Name	(2) Address	(3) Identifying number	(4) Check applicable box(es)		
			Category 1	Category 2	Constructive owner

F1 Name and address of foreign partnership	**2(a)** EIN (if any)
	2(b) Reference ID number (see instr.)
	3 Country under whose laws organized

4 Date of organization	**5** Principal place of business	**6** Principal business activity code number	**7** Principal business activity	**8a** Functional currency	**8b** Exchange rate (see instr.)

G Provide the following information for the foreign partnership's tax year:

1 Name, address, and identifying number of agent (if any) in the United States	**2** Check if the foreign partnership must file: ☐ Form 1042 ☐ Form 8804 ☐ Form 1065 or 1065-B Service Center where Form 1065 or 1065-B is filed:
3 Name and address of foreign partnership's agent in country of organization, if any	**4** Name and address of person(s) with custody of the books and records of the foreign partnership, and the location of such books and records, if different

5 Were any special allocations made by the foreign partnership? . . . . ► ☐ Yes ☐ No

6 Enter the number of Forms 8858, Information Return of U.S. Persons With Respect To Foreign Disregarded Entities, attached to this return (see instructions) . . . . ► _____

7 How is this partnership classified under the law of the country in which it is organized? . . ► _____

8 Did the partnership own any separate units within the meaning of Regulations section 1.1503-2(c)(3), (4), or 1.1503(d)-1(b)(4)? . . . . ► ☐ Yes ☐ No

9 Does this partnership meet **both** of the following requirements?
- The partnership's total receipts for the tax year were less than $250,000 and
- The value of the partnership's total assets at the end of the tax year was less than $1 million. } . . . . . . ► ☐ Yes ☐ No

If "Yes," **do not** complete Schedules L, M-1, and M-2.

Sign Here Only If You Are Filing This Form Separately and Not With Your Tax Return.	Under penalties of perjury, I declare that I have examined this return, including accompanying schedules and statements, and to the best of my knowledge and belief, it is true, correct, and complete. Declaration of preparer (other than general partner or limited liability company member) is based on all information of which preparer has any knowledge.
	► _____ ► _____
	Signature of general partner or limited liability company member Date

Paid Preparer Use Only	Print/Type preparer's name	Preparer's signature	Date	Check ☐ if self-employed	PTIN
	Firm's name ►			Firm's EIN ►	
	Firm's address ►			Phone no.	

For Privacy Act and Paperwork Reduction Act Notice, see the separate instructions.   Cat. No. 25852A   Form **8865** (2012)

Schedule A	**Constructive Ownership of Partnership Interest.** Check the boxes that apply to the filer. If you check box **b,** enter the name, address, and U.S. taxpayer identifying number (if any) of the person(s) whose interest you constructively own. See instructions.

a ☐ Owns a direct interest   **b** ☐ Owns a constructive interest

Name	Address	Identifying number (if any)	Check if foreign person	Check if direct partner

Schedule A-1	**Certain Partners of Foreign Partnership** (see instructions)

Name	Address	Identifying number (if any)	Check if foreign person

Does the partnership have any other foreign person as a direct partner? . . . . ☐ **Yes**   ☐ **No**

Schedule A-2	**Affiliation Schedule.** List all partnerships (foreign or domestic) in which the foreign partnership owns a direct interest or indirectly owns a 10% interest.

Name	Address	EIN (if any)	Total ordinary income or loss	Check if foreign partnership

Schedule B	**Income Statement—Trade or Business Income**

Caution. Include **only** trade or business income and expenses on lines 1a through 22 below. See the instructions for more information.

Income	**1a**	Gross receipts or sales	**1a**		
	b	Less returns and allowances	**1b**		**1c**
	2	Cost of goods sold			**2**
	3	Gross profit. Subtract line 2 from line 1c			**3**
	4	Ordinary income (loss) from other partnerships, estates, and trusts (attach statement) . . .			**4**
	5	Net farm profit (loss) (attach Schedule F (Form 1040))			**5**
	6	Net gain (loss) from Form 4797, Part II, line 17 (attach Form 4797)			**6**
	7	Other income (loss) (attach statement)			**7**
	8	**Total income (loss).** Combine lines 3 through 7			**8**
Deductions (see instructions for limitations)	**9**	Salaries and wages (other than to partners) (less employment credits)			**9**
	10	Guaranteed payments to partners			**10**
	11	Repairs and maintenance			**11**
	12	Bad debts			**12**
	13	Rent			**13**
	14	Taxes and licenses			**14**
	15	Interest			**15**
	16a	Depreciation (if required, attach Form 4562)	**16a**		
	b	Less depreciation reported elsewhere on return	**16b**		**16c**
	17	Depletion (**Do not** deduct oil and gas depletion.)			**17**
	18	Retirement plans, etc.			**18**
	19	Employee benefit programs			**19**
	20	Other deductions (attach statement)			**20**
	21	**Total deductions.** Add the amounts shown in the far right column for lines 9 through 20 . .			**21**
	22	**Ordinary business income (loss)** from trade or business activities. Subtract line 21 from line 8			**22**

Form **8865** (2012)

Schedule K	Partners' Distributive Share Items		Total amount

Income (Loss)

1	Ordinary business income (loss) (page 2, line 22)	1	
2	Net rental real estate income (loss) (attach Form 8825)	2	
3a	Other gross rental income (loss) — 3a		
b	Expenses from other rental activities (attach statement) — 3b		
c	Other net rental income (loss). Subtract line 3b from line 3a	3c	
4	Guaranteed payments	4	
5	Interest income	5	
6	Dividends: a Ordinary dividends	6a	
b	Qualified dividends — 6b		
7	Royalties	7	
8	Net short-term capital gain (loss) (attach Schedule D (Form 1065))	8	
9a	Net long-term capital gain (loss) (attach Schedule D (Form 1065))	9a	
b	Collectibles (28%) gain (loss) — 9b		
c	Unrecaptured section 1250 gain (attach statement) — 9c		
10	Net section 1231 gain (loss) (attach Form 4797)	10	
11	Other income (loss) (see instructions) Type ▶	11	

Deductions

12	Section 179 deduction (attach Form 4562)	12	
13a	Contributions	13a	
b	Investment interest expense	13b	
c	Section 59(e)(2) expenditures: (1) Type ▶ _____ (2) Amount ▶	13c(2)	
d	Other deductions (see instructions) Type ▶	13d	

Self-Employment

14a	Net earnings (loss) from self-employment	14a	
b	Gross farming or fishing income	14b	
c	Gross nonfarm income	14c	

Credits

15a	Low-income housing credit (section 42(j)(5))	15a	
b	Low-income housing credit (other)	15b	
c	Qualified rehabilitation expenditures (rental real estate) (attach Form 3468)	15c	
d	Other rental real estate credits (see instructions) Type ▶	15d	
e	Other rental credits (see instructions) Type ▶	15e	
f	Other credits (see instructions) Type ▶	15f	

Foreign Transactions

16a	Name of country or U.S. possession ▶		
b	Gross income from all sources	16b	
c	Gross income sourced at partner level	16c	
	Foreign gross income sourced at partnership level		
d	Passive category ▶ _____ e General category ▶ _____ f Other (attach statement) ▶	16f	
	Deductions allocated and apportioned at partner level		
g	Interest expense ▶ _____ h Other	16h	
	Deductions allocated and apportioned at partnership level to foreign source income		
i	Passive category ▶ _____ j General category ▶ _____ k Other (attach statement) ▶	16k	
l	Total foreign taxes (check one): ▶ ☐ Paid ☐ Accrued	16l	
m	Reduction in taxes available for credit (attach statement)	16m	
n	Other foreign tax information (attach statement)		

Alternative Minimum Tax (AMT) Items

17a	Post-1986 depreciation adjustment	17a	
b	Adjusted gain or loss	17b	
c	Depletion (other than oil and gas)	17c	
d	Oil, gas, and geothermal properties—gross income	17d	
e	Oil, gas, and geothermal properties—deductions	17e	
f	Other AMT items (attach statement)	17f	

Other Information

18a	Tax-exempt interest income	18a	
b	Other tax-exempt income	18b	
c	Nondeductible expenses	18c	
19a	Distributions of cash and marketable securities	19a	
b	Distributions of other property	19b	
20a	Investment income	20a	
b	Investment expenses	20b	
c	Other items and amounts (attach statement)		

Form **8865** (2012)

Schedule L	**Balance Sheets per Books.** (Not required if Item G9, page 1, is answered "Yes.")				
		Beginning of tax year		End of tax year	
	Assets	(a)	(b)	(c)	(d)
1	Cash				
2a	Trade notes and accounts receivable . . .				
b	Less allowance for bad debts				
3	Inventories				
4	U.S. government obligations				
5	Tax-exempt securities				
6	Other current assets (attach statement) . .				
7a	Loans to partners (or persons related to partners)				
b	Mortgage and real estate loans				
8	Other investments (attach statement) . . .				
9a	Buildings and other depreciable assets . .				
b	Less accumulated depreciation				
10a	Depletable assets				
b	Less accumulated depletion				
11	Land (net of any amortization)				
12a	Intangible assets (amortizable only) . . .				
b	Less accumulated amortization				
13	Other assets (attach statement)				
14	**Total** assets				
	Liabilities and Capital				
15	Accounts payable				
16	Mortgages, notes, bonds payable in less than 1 year				
17	Other current liabilities (attach statement) .				
18	All nonrecourse loans				
19a	Loans from partners (or persons related to partners)				
b	Mortgages, notes, bonds payable in 1 year or more				
20	Other liabilities (attach statement)				
21	Partners' capital accounts				
22	**Total** liabilities and capital				

Form **8865** (2012)

Schedule M	Balance Sheets for Interest Allocation		
		(a) Beginning of tax year	**(b)** End of tax year
1	Total U.S. assets		
2	Total foreign assets:		
a	Passive category		
b	General category		
c	Other (attach statement)		

Schedule M-1	Reconciliation of Income (Loss) per Books With Income (Loss) per Return. (Not required if Item G9, page 1, is answered "Yes.")		

1 Net income (loss) per books .		**6** Income recorded on books this year not included on Schedule K, lines 1 through 11 (itemize):	
2 Income included on Schedule K, lines 1, 2, 3c, 5, 6a, 7, 8, 9a, 10, and 11 not recorded on books this year (itemize):		**a** Tax-exempt interest $ _____	
3 Guaranteed payments (other than health insurance) . . .		**7** Deductions included on Schedule K, lines 1 through 13d, and 16l not charged against book income this year (itemize):	
4 Expenses recorded on books this year not included on Schedule K, lines 1 through 13d, and 16l (itemize):		**a** Depreciation $ _____	
a Depreciation $ _____			
b Travel and entertainment $ _____		**8** Add lines 6 and 7	
5 Add lines 1 through 4 . . .		**9** Income (loss). Subtract line 8 from line 5	

Schedule M-2	Analysis of Partners' Capital Accounts. (Not required if Item G9, page 1, is answered "Yes.")		
1 Balance at beginning of year		**6** Distributions: **a** Cash . . .	
2 Capital contributed:		**b** Property . .	
a Cash . . .		**7** Other decreases (itemize): _____	
b Property . .			
3 Net income (loss) per books .			
4 Other increases (itemize): _____		**8** Add lines 6 and 7	
		9 Balance at end of year. Subtract line 8 from line 5	
5 Add lines 1 through 4 . . .			

Form **8865** (2012)

| Schedule N | Transactions Between Controlled Foreign Partnership and Partners or Other Related Entities |

Important: Complete a separate Form 8865 and Schedule N for each controlled foreign partnership. Enter the totals for each type of transaction that occurred between the foreign partnership and the persons listed in columns (a) through (d).

Transactions of foreign partnership	(a) U.S. person filing this return	(b) Any domestic corporation or partnership controlling or controlled by the U.S. person filing this return	(c) Any other foreign corporation or partnership controlling or controlled by the U.S. person filing this return	(d) Any U.S. person with a 10% or more direct interest in the controlled foreign partnership (other than the U.S. person filing this return)
1 Sales of inventory				
2 Sales of property rights (patents, trademarks, etc.)				
3 Compensation received for technical, managerial, engineering, construction, or like services				
4 Commissions received				
5 Rents, royalties, and license fees received				
6 Distributions received				
7 Interest received				
8 Other				
9 Add lines 1 through 8				
10 Purchases of inventory				
11 Purchases of tangible property other than inventory				
12 Purchases of property rights (patents, trademarks, etc.)				
13 Compensation paid for technical, managerial, engineering, construction, or like services				
14 Commissions paid				
15 Rents, royalties, and license fees paid				
16 Distributions paid				
17 Interest paid				
18 Other				
19 Add lines 10 through 18				
20 Amounts borrowed (enter the maximum loan balance during the year). See instructions				
21 Amounts loaned (enter the maximum loan balance during the year). See instructions				

Form **8865** (2012)

Form 8891

Form **8891** (Rev. December 2012)	**U.S. Information Return for Beneficiaries of Certain Canadian Registered Retirement Plans** ▶ Attach to Form 1040.	OMB No. 1545-0074
Department of the Treasury Internal Revenue Service	For calendar year 20_____ , or tax year beginning _____ , 20 _____ , and ending _____ , 20 _____ . ▶ **Information about Form 8891 and its instructions is at** *www.irs.gov/form8891.*	Attachment Sequence No. **139**

Name as shown on Form 1040	Identifying number (see instructions)

Address

1 Name of plan custodian

2 Account number of plan

3 Address of plan custodian

4 Type of plan (check one box):
☐ Registered Retirement Savings Plan (RRSP)
☐ Registered Retirement Income Fund (RRIF)

5 Check the applicable box for your status in the plan (see *Definitions* in the instructions):
☐ Beneficiary
☐ Annuitant (Complete only lines 7a, 7b, and 8.)

6a Have you previously made an election under Article XVIII(7) of the U.S.-Canada income tax treaty to defer U.S. income tax on the undistributed earnings of the plan? . . . . ▶ ☐ Yes ☐ No

b If "Yes," enter the first year the election came into effect _____ and go to line 7a. If "No," go to line 6c.

c If you have not previously made the election described on line 6a above, you can make an irrevocable election for this year and subsequent years by checking this box . . . . ▶ ☐

7a Distributions received from the plan during the year. Enter here and include on Form 1040, line 16a	**7a**	
b Taxable distributions received from the plan during the year. Enter here and include on Form 1040, line 16b	**7b**	
8 Plan balance at the end of the year. If you checked the "Annuitant" box on line 5, the "Yes" box on line 6a, or the box on line 6c, **stop here. Do not** complete the rest of the form	**8**	
9 Contributions to the plan during the year	**9**	
10 **Undistributed earnings of the plan during the year:**		
a Interest income. Enter here and include on Form 1040, line 8a	**10a**	
b Total ordinary dividends. Enter here and include on Form 1040, line 9a	**10b**	
c Qualified dividends. Enter here and include on Form 1040, line 9b	**10c**	
d Capital gains. Enter here and include on Form 1040, line 13	**10d**	
e Other income. Enter here and include on Form 1040, line 21. List type and amount ▶ _____	**10e**	

For Paperwork Reduction Act Notice, see instructions.	Cat. No. 37699X	Form **8891** (Rev. 12-2012)

Section references are to the Internal Revenue Code.

Future Developments

For the latest information about developments related to Form 8891 and its instructions, such as legislation enacted after they were published, go to *www.irs.gov/form8891*.

General Instructions

Purpose of Form

Form 8891 is used by U.S. citizens or residents (a) to report contributions to Canadian registered retirement savings plans (RRSPs) and registered retirement income funds (RRIFs), (b) to report undistributed earnings in RRSPs and RRIFs, and (c) to report distributions received from RRSPs and RRIFs. See Notice 2003-75, which is available at IRS.gov.

Form 8891 also can be used to make an election pursuant to Article XVIII(7) of the U.S.-Canada income tax treaty to defer U.S. income tax on income earned by an RRSP or an RRIF that has been accrued, but not distributed. Taxpayers who have not previously made the election can make it on this form by checking the box on line 6c.

Who Must File

Form 8891 must be completed and attached to Form 1040 by any U.S. citizen or resident who is a beneficiary of an RRSP or RRIF. Do **not** file Form 8891 by itself.

A U.S. citizen or resident who is an annuitant of an RRSP or RRIF must file the form for any year in which he or she receives a distribution from the RRSP or RRIF.

A separate Form 8891 must be filed for each RRSP or RRIF for which there is a filing requirement. If you and your spouse are both required to file Form 8891, each of you must complete and attach a separate Form 8891 to Form 1040, even if you file a joint return.

Definitions

Beneficiary. A beneficiary of an RRSP or RRIF is an individual who is subject to current U.S. income taxation on income accrued in the RRSP or RRIF or would be subject to current income taxation had the individual not made the election under Article XVIII(7) of the U.S.-Canada income tax treaty to defer U.S. income taxation of income accrued in the RRSP or RRIF.

Annuitant. For purposes of this form, an annuitant of an RRSP or RRIF is an individual who is designated pursuant to the RRSP or RRIF as an annuitant and is not also a beneficiary as defined above.

Record Retention

Taxpayers must retain supporting documentation relating to the information reported on Form 8891, including Canadian forms T4RSP, T4RIF, or NR4, and periodic or annual statements issued by the custodian of the RRSP or RRIF.

Other Reporting Requirements

Pursuant to section 6048(d)(4), annuitants and beneficiaries who are required to file Form 8891 will not be required to file Form 3520 and will not be subject to the associated penalties described in section 6677 on such RRSPs or RRIFs.

You may be required to file Form TD F 90-22.1, Report of Foreign Bank and Financial Accounts. You may also be required to file Form 8938, Statement of Specified Foreign Financial Assets, for other Canadian assets not reported on this Form 8891. For more information, see the instructions for Schedule B (Form 1040A or 1040) at *www.irs.gov/form1040,* and the instructions for Form 8938 at *www.irs.gov/form8938.*

Specific Instructions

All amounts listed must be in U.S. dollars.

Name and Address

Enter your name and address as shown on Form 1040. Even if you are filing a joint Form 1040 with your spouse, enter only your name.

Identifying number

Enter your U.S. social security number (SSN) or individual taxpayer identification number (ITIN). Do not enter a Canadian identifying number.

Beneficiaries

A beneficiary who previously made the election to defer income on the plan or is making it initially by checking the box on line 6c must only complete lines 1 through 8 of the form.

Annuitants

If you are treated as an annuitant for purposes of this form (see *Definitions*), you should complete only lines 1 through 5, 7a, 7b, and 8.

Line 6(a)

If the election you made previously was made under Rev. Proc. 89-45, check the "No" box. If an election (other than an election under Rev. Proc. 89-45) was made for an RRSP, and amounts from the RRSP were rolled over tax-free to an RRIF or another RRSP, the election is considered to have been made for the plan which received the tax-free rollover.

Line 6(c)

If you did not make the election under Article XVIII to defer income tax on income earned by an RRSP or an RRIF in a previous year, you cannot make a late election on Form 8891. However, you may be able to seek relief from the IRS for failure to timely elect the deferral of income on Form 8891 in an earlier year.

Line 7(b)

For information on figuring taxable distributions, see section 72 and Pub. 939, General Rule for Pensions and Annuities.

Paperwork Reduction Act Notice

We ask for the information on this form to carry out the Internal Revenue laws of the United States. You are required to give us the information. We need it to ensure that you are complying with these laws and to allow us to figure and collect the right amount of tax.

You are not required to provide the information requested on a form that is subject to the Paperwork Reduction Act unless the form displays a valid OMB control number. Books or records relating to a form or its instructions must be retained as long as their contents may become material in the administration of any Internal Revenue law. Generally, tax returns and return information are confidential, as required by Internal Revenue Code section 6103.

The average time and expenses required to complete and file this form will vary depending on individual circumstances. For the estimated averages, see the instructions for your income tax return.

If you have suggestions for making this form simpler, we would be happy to hear from you. See the instructions for your income tax return.

Form 8938

Form **8938**
(November 2012)

Department of the Treasury
Internal Revenue Service

Statement of Specified Foreign Financial Assets

▶ Information about Form 8938 and its separate instructions is at *www.irs.gov/form8938*.
▶ Attach to your tax return

OMB No. 1545-2195

Attachment
Sequence No. **175**

If you have attached additional sheets, check here ☐

Name(s) shown on return	Identifying number

Number, street, and room or suite no. (if a P.O. box, see instructions)

City or town, province or state, and country (including postal code)

For tax year beginning _____, 20____, and ending _____, 20____

Note. All information must be in English. Show all amounts in U.S. dollars. Show currency conversion rates in Part I, line 6(2), or Part II, line 6(2).

Type of filer

a Specified individual   **(1)** ☐ Married filing a joint return   **(2)** ☐ Married filing a separate return   **(3)** ☐ Other individual

b Specified domestic entity   **(1)** ☐ Partnership   **(2)** ☐ Corporation   **(3)** ☐ Trust

Check this box if this is an amended or supplemental Form 8938 for the tax year . . . . ☐

Part I   Foreign Deposit and Custodial Accounts (see instructions)

If you have more than one account to report, attach a continuation sheet with the same information for each additional account (see instructions).

1	Type of account ☐ Deposit ☐ Custodial	**2**	Account number or other designation

3   Check all that apply   **a** ☐ Account opened during tax year   **b** ☐ Account closed during tax year
     c ☐ Account jointly owned with spouse   **d** ☐ No tax item reported in Part III with respect to this account

4   Maximum value of account during tax year . . . . $

5   Did you use a foreign currency exchange rate to convert the value of the account into U.S. dollars? . . ☐ Yes   ☐ No

6   If you answered "Yes" to line 5, complete all that apply.

(1) Foreign currency in which account is maintained	**(2)** Foreign currency exchange rate used to convert to U.S. dollars	**(3)** Source of exchange rate used if not from U.S. Treasury Financial Management Service

7   Name of financial institution in which account is maintained

8   Mailing address of financial institution in which account is maintained. Number, street, and room or suite no.

9   City or town, province or state, and country (including postal code)

Part II   Other Foreign Assets (see instructions)

Note. *If you reported specified foreign financial assets on Forms 3520, 3520-A, 5471, 8621, 8865, or 8891 you do not have to include the assets on Form 8938. You must complete Part IV. See instructions.*

If you have more than one asset to report, attach a continuation sheet with the same information for each additional asset (see instructions).

1	Description of asset	**2**	Identifying number or other designation

3   Complete all that apply. See instructions for reporting of multiple acquisition or disposition dates.

   a   Date asset acquired during tax year, if applicable . . . . _____

   b   Date asset disposed of during tax year, if applicable . . . . _____

   c ☐ Check if asset jointly owned with spouse   **d** ☐ Check if no tax item reported in Part III with respect to this asset

4   Maximum value of asset during tax year (check box that applies)

   a ☐ $0 - $50,000   **b** ☐ $50,001 - $100,000   **c** ☐ $100,001 - $150,000   **d** ☐ $150,001 - $200,000

   e   If more than $200,000, list value . . . . $

5   Did you use a foreign currency exchange rate to convert the value of the asset into U.S. dollars? . . . ☐ Yes   ☐ No

For Paperwork Reduction Act Notice, see the separate instructions.   Cat. No. 37753A   Form **8938** (11-2012)

Part II Other Foreign Assets *(continued)*

6 If you answered "Yes" to line 5, complete all that apply.

(1) Foreign currency in which asset is denominated	(2) Foreign currency exchange rate used to convert to U.S. dollars	(3) Source of exchange rate used if not from U.S. Treasury Financial Management Service

7 If asset reported in Part II, line 1, is stock of a foreign entity or an interest in a foreign entity, report the following information.

a Name of foreign entity _____

b Type of foreign entity   (1)☐ Partnership   (2)☐ Corporation   (3)☐ Trust   (4)☐ Estate

c Mailing address of foreign entity. Number, street, and room or suite no.

_____

d City or town, province or state, and country (including postal code)

8 If asset reported in Part II, line 1, is not stock of a foreign entity or an interest in a foreign entity, report the following information for the asset.

   Note. If this asset has more than one issuer or counterparty, attach a continuation sheet with the same information for each additional issuer or counterparty (see instructions).

a Name of issuer or counterparty _____
   Check if information is for   ☐ Issuer   ☐ Counterparty

b Type of issuer or counterparty
   (1)☐ Individual   (2)☐ Partnership   (3)☐ Corporation   (4)☐ Trust   (5)☐ Estate

c Check if issuer or counterparty is a   ☐ U.S. person   ☐ Foreign person

d Mailing address of issuer or counterparty. Number, street, and room or suite no.

_____

e City or town, province or state, and country (including postal code)

Part III Summary of Tax Items Attributable to Specified Foreign Financial Assets *(see instructions)*

Asset Category	Tax item	Amount reported on form or schedule	Where reported	
			Form and line	Schedule and line
I. Foreign Deposit and Custodial Accounts	a Interest	$		
	b Dividends	$		
	c Royalties	$		
	d Other income	$		
	e Gains (losses)	$		
	f Deductions	$		
	g Credits	$		
II. Other Foreign Assets	a Interest	$		
	b Dividends	$		
	c Royalties	$		
	d Other income	$		
	e Gains (losses)	$		
	f Deductions	$		
	g Credits	$		

Part IV Excepted Specified Foreign Financial Assets *(see instructions)*

If you reported specified foreign financial assets on the following forms, check the appropriate box(es). Indicate number of forms filed. You do not need to include these assets on Form 8938 for the tax year.

☐ 3520   Number of forms _____   ☐ 3520-A Number of forms _____   ☐ 5471 Number of forms _____
☐ 8621   Number of forms _____   ☐ 8865   Number of forms _____   ☐ 8891 Number of forms _____

Form **8938** (11-2012)

Form TDF 90-221

TD F 90-22.1
(Rev. January 2012)
Department of the Treasury

Do not use previous editions of this form

REPORT OF FOREIGN BANK AND FINANCIAL ACCOUNTS

Do NOT file with your Federal Tax Return

OMB No. 1545-2038

1 This Report is for Calendar Year Ended 12/31

_____ ___ ___ ____

Amended ☐

Part I Filer Information

2 Type of Filer

a ☐ Individual   b ☐ Partnership   c ☐ Corporation   d ☐ Consolidated   e ☐ Fiduciary or Other—Enter type _____

3 U.S. Taxpayer Identification Number

If filer has no U.S. Identification Number complete Item 4.

4 Foreign identification (Complete only if item 3 is not applicable.)

a Type: ☐ Passport   ☐ Other _____

b Number

c Country of Issue

5 Individual's Date of Birth MM/DD/YYYY

6 Last Name or Organization Name

7 First Name

8 Middle Initial

9 Address (Number, Street, and Apt. or Suite No.)

10 City

11 State

12 Zip/Postal Code

13 Country

14 Does the filer have a financial interest in 25 or more financial accounts?

☐ Yes   If "Yes" enter total number of accounts _____

(If "Yes" is checked, do not complete Part II or Part III, but retain records of this information)

☐ No

Part II Information on Financial Account(s) Owned Separately

15 Maximum value of account during calendar year reported

16 Type of account   a ☐ Bank   b ☐ Securities   c ☐ Other—Enter type below

17 Name of Financial Institution in which account is held

18 Account number or other designation

19 Mailing Address (Number, Street, Suite Number) of financial institution in which account is held

20 City

21 State, if known

22 Zip/Postal Code, if known

23 Country

Signature

44 Filer Signature

45 Filer Title, if not reporting a personal account

46 Date (MM/DD/YYYY)

File this form with: U.S. Department of the Treasury, P.O. Box 32621, Detroit, MI 48232-0621

This form should be used to report a financial interest in, signature authority, or other authority over one or more financial accounts in foreign countries, as required by the Department of the Treasury Regulations 31 CFR 1010.350 (formerly 31 CFR 103.24). No report is required if the aggregate value of the accounts did not exceed $10,000. **See Instructions For Definitions.**

PRIVACY ACT AND PAPERWORK REDUCTION ACT NOTICE

Pursuant to the requirements of Public Law 93-579 (Privacy Act of 1974), notice is hereby given that the authority to collect information on TD F 90-22.1 in accordance with 5 USC 552a (e) is Public Law 91-508; 31 USC 5314; 5 USC 301; 31 CFR 1010.350 (formerly 31 CFR 103.24).

The principal purpose for collecting the information is to assure maintenance of reports where such reports or records have a high degree of usefulness in criminal, tax, or regulatory investigations or proceedings. The information collected may be provided to those officers and employees of any constituent unit of the Department of the Treasury who have a need for the records in the performance of their duties. The records may be referred to any other department or agency of the United States upon the request of the head of such department or agency for use in a criminal, tax, or regulatory investigation or proceeding. The information collected may also be provided to appropriate state, local, and foreign law enforcement and regulatory personnel in the performance of their official duties. Disclosure of this information is mandatory. Civil and criminal penalties, including in certain circumstances a fine of not more than $500,000 and imprisonment of not more than five years, are provided for failure to file a report, supply information, and for filing a false or fraudulent report. Disclosure of the Social Security number is mandatory. The authority to collect is 31 CFR 1010.350 (formerly 31 CFR 103.24) . The Social Security number will be used as a means to identify the individual who files the report.

The estimated average burden associated with this collection of information is 75 minutes per respondent or record keeper, depending on individual circumstances. Comments regarding the accuracy of this burden estimate, and suggestions for reducing the burden should be directed to the Internal Revenue Service, Bank Secrecy Act Policy, 5000 Ellin Road C-3-242, Lanham MD 20706.

Cat. No. 12996D

Form **TD F 90-22.1** (Rev. 1-2012)

Complete a Separate Block for Each Account Owned Separately

This side can be copied as many times as necessary in order to provide information on all accounts.

1 Filing for calendar year ____ ____ ____ ____	**3–4** Check appropriate Identification Number ☐ Taxpayer Identification Number ☐ Foreign Identification Number Enter identification number here:	**6** Last Name or Organization Name

15 Maximum value of account during calendar year reported	**16** Type of account **a** ☐ Bank **b** ☐ Securities **c** ☐ Other—Enter type below

17 Name of Financial Institution in which account is held

18 Account number or other designation	**19** Mailing Address (Number, Street, Suite Number) of financial institution in which account is held

20 City	**21** State, if known	**22** Zip/Postal Code, if known	**23** Country

15 Maximum value of account during calendar year reported	**16** Type of account **a** ☐ Bank **b** ☐ Securities **c** ☐ Other—Enter type below

17 Name of Financial Institution in which account is held

18 Account number or other designation	**19** Mailing Address (Number, Street, Suite Number) of financial institution in which account is held

20 City	**21** State, if known	**22** Zip/Postal Code, if known	**23** Country

15 Maximum value of account during calendar year reported	**16** Type of account **a** ☐ Bank **b** ☐ Securities **c** ☐ Other—Enter type below

17 Name of Financial Institution in which account is held

18 Account number or other designation	**19** Mailing Address (Number, Street, Suite Number) of financial institution in which account is held

20 City	**21** State, if known	**22** Zip/Postal Code, if known	**23** Country

15 Maximum value of account during calendar year reported	**16** Type of account **a** ☐ Bank **b** ☐ Securities **c** ☐ Other—Enter type below

17 Name of Financial Institution in which account is held

18 Account number or other designation	**19** Mailing Address (Number, Street, Suite Number) of financial institution in which account is held

20 City	**21** State, if known	**22** Zip/Postal Code, if known	**23** Country

15 Maximum value of account during calendar year reported	**16** Type of account **a** ☐ Bank **b** ☐ Securities **c** ☐ Other—Enter type below

17 Name of Financial Institution in which account is held

18 Account number or other designation	**19** Mailing Address (Number, Street, Suite Number) of financial institution in which account is held

20 City	**21** State, if known	**22** Zip/Postal Code, if known	**23** Country

15 Maximum value of account during calendar year reported	**16** Type of account **a** ☐ Bank **b** ☐ Securities **c** ☐ Other—Enter type below

17 Name of Financial Institution in which account is held

18 Account number or other designation	**19** Mailing Address (Number, Street, Suite Number) of financial institution in which account is held

20 City	**21** State, if known	**22** Zip/Postal Code, if known	**23** Country

Form **TD F 90-22.1** (Rev. 1-2012)

General Instructions

Form TD F 90-22.1, Report of Foreign Bank and Financial Accounts (the "FBAR"), is used to report a financial interest in or signature authority over a foreign financial account. The FBAR must be **received** by the Department of the Treasury on or before **June 30th** of the year immediately following the calendar year being reported. The June 30th filing date may not be extended.

Who Must File an FBAR. A United States person that has a financial interest in or signature authority over foreign financial accounts must file an FBAR if the aggregate value of the foreign financial accounts exceeds $10,000 at any time during the calendar year. See General Definitions, to determine who is a United States person.

General Definitions

Financial Account. A financial account includes, but is not limited to, a securities, brokerage, savings, demand, checking, deposit, time deposit, or other account maintained with a financial institution (or other person performing the services of a financial institution). A financial account also includes a commodity futures or options account, an insurance policy with a cash value (such as a whole life insurance policy), an annuity policy with a cash value, and shares in a mutual fund or similar pooled fund (i.e., a fund that is available to the general public with a regular net asset value determination and regular redemptions).

Foreign Financial Account. A foreign financial account is a financial account located outside of the United States. For example, an account maintained with a branch of a United States bank that is physically located outside of the United States is a foreign financial account. An account maintained with a branch of a foreign bank that is physically located in the United States is not a foreign financial account.

Financial Interest. A United States person has a financial interest in a foreign financial account for which:

(1) the United States person is the owner of record or holder of legal title, regardless of whether the account is maintained for the benefit of the United States person or for the benefit of another person; or

(2) the owner of record or holder of legal title is one of the following:

(a) An agent, nominee, attorney, or a person acting in some other capacity on behalf of the United States person with respect to the account;

(b) A corporation in which the United States person owns directly or indirectly: **(i)** more than 50 percent of the total value of shares of stock or **(ii)** more than 50 percent of the voting power of all shares of stock;

(c) A partnership in which the United States person owns directly or indirectly: **(i)** an interest in more than 50 percent of the partnership's profits (e.g., distributive share of partnership income taking into account any special allocation agreement) or **(ii)** an interest in more than 50 percent of the partnership capital;

(d) A trust of which the United States person: **(i)** is the trust grantor and **(ii)** has an ownership interest in the trust for United States federal tax purposes. See 26 U.S.C. sections 671-679 to determine if a grantor has an ownership interest in a trust;

(e) A trust in which the United States person has a greater than 50 percent present beneficial interest in the assets or income of the trust for the calendar year; or

(f) Any other entity in which the United States person owns directly or indirectly more than 50 percent of the voting power, total value of equity interest or assets, or interest in profits.

Person. A person means an individual and legal entities including, but not limited to, a limited liability company, corporation, partnership, trust, and estate.

Signature Authority. Signature authority is the authority of an individual (alone or in conjunction with another individual) to control the disposition of assets held in a foreign financial account by direct communication (whether in writing or otherwise) to the bank or other financial institution that maintains the financial account. See Exceptions, Signature Authority.

United States. For FBAR purposes, the United States includes the States, the District of Columbia, all United States territories and possessions (e.g., American Samoa, the Commonwealth of the Northern Mariana Islands, the Commonwealth of Puerto Rico, Guam, and the United States Virgin Islands), and the Indian lands as defined in the Indian Gaming Regulatory Act. References to the laws of the United States include the laws of the United States federal government and the laws of all places listed in this definition.

United States Person. United States person means United States citizens; United States residents; entities, including but not limited to, corporations, partnerships, or limited liability companies created or organized in the United States or under the laws of the United States; and trusts or estates formed under the laws of the United States.

Note. The federal tax treatment of an entity does not determine whether the entity has an FBAR filing requirement. For example, an entity that is disregarded for purposes of Title 26 of the United States Code must file an FBAR, if otherwise required to do so. Similarly, a trust for which the trust income, deductions, or credits are taken into account by another person for purposes of Title 26 of the United States Code must file an FBAR, if otherwise required to do so.

United States Resident. A United States resident is an alien residing in the United States. To determine if the filer is a resident of the United States apply the residency tests in 26 U.S.C. section 7701(b). When applying the residency tests, use the definition of United States in these instructions.

Exceptions

Certain Accounts Jointly Owned by Spouses. The spouse of an individual who files an FBAR is not required to file a separate FBAR if the following conditions are met: **(1)** all the financial accounts that the non-filing spouse is required to report are jointly owned with the filing spouse; **(2)** the filing spouse reports the jointly owned accounts on a timely filed FBAR; and **(3)** both spouses sign the FBAR in Item 44. See Explanations for Specific Items, Part III, Items 25-33. Otherwise, both spouses are required to file separate FBARs, and each spouse must report the entire value of the jointly owned accounts.

Consolidated FBAR. If a United States person that is an entity is named in a consolidated FBAR filed by a greater than 50 percent owner, such entity is not required to file a separate FBAR. See Explanations for Specific Items, Part V.

Correspondent/Nostro Account. Correspondent or nostro accounts (which are maintained by banks and used solely for bank-to-bank settlements) are not required to be reported.

Governmental Entity. A foreign financial account of any governmental entity of the United States (as defined above) is not required to be reported by any person. For purposes of this form, governmental entity includes a college or university that is an agency of, an instrumentality of, owned by, or operated by a governmental entity. For purposes of this form, governmental entity also includes an employee retirement or welfare benefit plan of a governmental entity.

International Financial Institution. A foreign financial account of any international financial institution (if the United States government is a member) is not required to be reported by any person.

IRA Owners and Beneficiaries. An owner or beneficiary of an IRA is not required to report a foreign financial account held in the IRA.

Participants in and Beneficiaries of Tax-Qualified Retirement Plans. A participant in or beneficiary of a retirement plan described in Internal Revenue Code section 401(a), 403(a), or 403(b) is not required to report a foreign financial account held by or on behalf of the retirement plan.

Signature Authority. Individuals who have signature authority over, but no financial interest in, a foreign financial account are not required to report the account in the following situations:

(1) An officer or employee of a bank that is examined by the Office of the Comptroller of the Currency, the Board of Governors of the Federal Reserve System, the Federal Deposit Insurance Corporation, the Office of Thrift Supervision, or the National Credit Union Administration is not required to report signature authority over a foreign financial account owned or maintained by the bank.

(2) An officer or employee of a financial institution that is registered with and examined by the Securities and Exchange Commission or Commodity Futures Trading Commission is not required to report signature authority over a foreign financial account owned or maintained by the financial institution.

(3) An officer or employee of an Authorized Service Provider is not required to report signature authority over a foreign financial account that is owned or maintained by an investment company that is registered with the Securities and Exchange Commission. Authorized Service Provider means an entity that is registered with and examined by the Securities and Exchange Commission and provides services to an investment company registered under the Investment Company Act of 1940.

(4) An officer or employee of an entity that has a class of equity securities listed (or American depository receipts listed) on any United States national securities exchange is not required to report signature authority over a foreign financial account of such entity.

(5) An officer or employee of a United States subsidiary is not required to report signature authority over a foreign financial account of the subsidiary if its United States parent has a class of equity securities listed on any United States national securities exchange and the subsidiary is included in a consolidated FBAR report of the United States parent.

(6) An officer or employee of an entity that has a class of equity securities registered (or American depository receipts in respect of equity securities registered) under section 12(g) of the Securities Exchange Act is not required to report signature authority over a foreign financial account of such entity.

Trust Beneficiaries. A trust beneficiary with a financial interest described in section (2)(e) of the financial interest definition is not required to report the trust's foreign financial accounts on an FBAR if the trust, trustee of the trust, or agent of the trust: **(1)** is a United States person and **(2)** files an FBAR disclosing the trust's foreign financial accounts.

United States Military Banking Facility. A financial account maintained with a financial institution located on a United States military installation is not required to be reported, even if that military installation is outside of the United States.

Filing Information

When and Where to File. The FBAR is an annual report and must be **received** by the Department of the Treasury **on or before June 30th** of the year following the calendar year being reported. **Do Not file with federal income tax return.**

File by mailing to:

Department of the Treasury
Post Office Box 32621
Detroit, MI 48232-0621

If an express delivery service is used, file by mailing to:

IRS Enterprise Computing Center
ATTN: CTR Operations Mailroom, 4th Floor
985 Michigan Avenue
Detroit, MI 48226

The FBAR may be hand delivered to any local office of the Internal Revenue Service for forwarding to the Department of the Treasury, Detroit, MI. The FBAR may also be delivered to the Internal Revenue Service's tax attaches located in United States embassies and consulates for forwarding to the Department of the Treasury, Detroit, MI. The FBAR is not considered filed until it is received by the Department of the Treasury in Detroit, MI.

No Extension of Time to File. There is no extension of time available for filing an FBAR. Extensions of time to file federal tax returns do NOT extend the time for filing an FBAR. If a delinquent FBAR is filed, attach a statement explaining the reason for the late filing.

Amending a Previously Filed FBAR. To amend a filed FBAR, check the "Amended" box in the upper right hand corner of the first page of the FBAR. Complete the form in its entirety and include the amended information. Do not attach a copy of the original FBAR. An amendment should not be made until at least **120** calendar days after the original FBAR is filed.

Record Keeping Requirements. Persons required to file an FBAR must retain records that contain the name in which each account is maintained, the number or other designation of the account, the name and address of the foreign financial institution that maintains the account, the type of account, and the maximum account value of each account during the reporting period. The records must be retained for a period of 5 years from June 30th of the year following the calendar year reported and must be available for inspection as provided by law. Retaining a copy of the filed FBAR can help to satisfy the record keeping requirements.

An officer or employee who files an FBAR to report signature authority over an employer's foreign financial account is not required to personally retain records regarding these accounts.

Questions. FBAR help is available by telephone or e-mail. Call 866-270-0733 (toll-free within the U.S.) or 313-234-6146 (from outside the U.S., not toll-free) from 8 a.m.—4:30 p.m. Eastern time, or e-mail your inquiry to FBARquestions@irs.gov.

Explanations for Specific Items

Part I — Filer Information

Item 1. The FBAR is an annual report. Enter the calendar year being reported. If amending a previously filed FBAR, check the "Amended" box.

Item 2. Check the box that describes the filer. Check only one box. Individuals reporting only signature authority, check box "a". If filing a consolidated FBAR, check box "d". To determine if a consolidated FBAR can be filed, see Part V. If the type of filer is not listed in boxes "a" through "c", check box "e", and enter the type of filer. Persons that should check box "e" include, but are not limited to, trusts, estates, limited liability companies, and tax-exempt entities (even if the entity is organized as a corporation). A disregarded entity must check box "e", and enter the type of entity followed by "(D.E.)". For example, a limited liability company that is disregarded for United States federal tax purposes would enter "limited liability company (D.E.)".

Item 3. Provide the filer's United States taxpayer identification number. Generally, this is the filer's United States social security number (SSN), United States individual taxpayer identification number (ITIN), or employer identification number (EIN). Throughout the FBAR, numbers should be entered with no spaces, dashes, or other punctuation. If the filer does NOT have a United States taxpayer identification number, complete Item 4.

Item 4. Complete Item 4 only if the filer does NOT have a United States taxpayer identification number. Item 4 requires the filer to provide information from an official foreign government document to verify the filer's nationality or residence. Enter the document number followed by the country of issuance, check the appropriate type of document, and if "other" is checked, provide the type of document.

Item 5. If the filer is an individual, enter the filer's date of birth, using the month, day, and year convention.

Items 9, 10, 11, 12, and 13. Enter the filer's address. An individual residing in the United States must enter the street address of the individual's United States residence, not a post office box. An individual residing outside the United States must enter the individual's United States mailing address. If the individual does not have a United States mailing address, the individual must enter a foreign residence address. An entity must enter its United States mailing address. If the entity does not have a United States mailing address, the entity must enter its foreign mailing address.

Item 14. If the filer has a financial interest in 25 or more foreign financial accounts, check "Yes" and enter the number of accounts. Do not complete Part II or Part III of the FBAR. If filing a consolidated FBAR, only complete Part V, Items 34-42, for each United States entity included in the consolidated FBAR.

Note. If the filer has signature authority over 25 or more foreign financial accounts, only complete Part IV, Items 34-43, for each person for which the filer has signature authority, and check "No" in Part I, Item 14.

Filers must comply with applicable recording keeping requirements. See Record Keeping Requirements.

Part II — Information on Financial Account(s) Owned Separately

Enter information in the applicable parts of the form only. Number the pages used, and mail only those pages. If there is not enough space to provide all account information, copy and complete additional pages of the required Part as necessary. Do not use any attachments unless otherwise specified in the instructions.

(3) An officer or employee of an Authorized Service Provider is not required to report signature authority over a foreign financial account that is owned or maintained by an investment company that is registered with the Securities and Exchange Commission. Authorized Service Provider means an entity that is registered with and examined by the Securities and Exchange Commission and provides services to an investment company registered under the Investment Company Act of 1940.

(4) An officer or employee of an entity that has a class of equity securities listed (or American depository receipts listed) on any United States national securities exchange is not required to report signature authority over a foreign financial account of such entity.

(5) An officer or employee of a United States subsidiary is not required to report signature authority over a foreign financial account of the subsidiary if its United States parent has a class of equity securities listed on any United States national securities exchange and the subsidiary is included in a consolidated FBAR report of the United States parent.

(6) An officer or employee of an entity that has a class of equity securities registered (or American depository receipts in respect of equity securities registered) under section 12(g) of the Securities Exchange Act is not required to report signature authority over a foreign financial account of such entity.

Trust Beneficiaries. A trust beneficiary with a financial interest described in section (2)(e) of the financial interest definition is not required to report the trust's foreign financial accounts on an FBAR if the trust, trustee of the trust, or agent of the trust: **(1)** is a United States person and **(2)** files an FBAR disclosing the trust's foreign financial accounts.

United States Military Banking Facility. A financial account maintained with a financial institution located on a United States military installation is not required to be reported, even if that military installation is outside of the United States.

Filing Information

When and Where to File. The FBAR is an annual report and must be **received** by the Department of the Treasury **on or before June 30th** of the year following the calendar year being reported. **Do Not file with federal income tax return.**

File by mailing to:

Department of the Treasury
Post Office Box 32621
Detroit, MI 48232-0621

If an express delivery service is used, file by mailing to:

IRS Enterprise Computing Center
ATTN: CTR Operations Mailroom, 4th Floor
985 Michigan Avenue
Detroit, MI 48226

The FBAR may be hand delivered to any local office of the Internal Revenue Service for forwarding to the Department of the Treasury, Detroit, MI. The FBAR may also be delivered to the Internal Revenue Service's tax attaches located in United States embassies and consulates for forwarding to the Department of the Treasury, Detroit, MI. The FBAR is not considered filed until it is received by the Department of the Treasury in Detroit, MI.

No Extension of Time to File. There is no extension of time available for filing an FBAR. Extensions of time to file federal tax returns do NOT extend the time for filing an FBAR. If a delinquent FBAR is filed, attach a statement explaining the reason for the late filing.

Amending a Previously Filed FBAR. To amend a filed FBAR, check the "Amended" box in the upper right hand corner of the first page of the FBAR. Complete the form in its entirety and include the amended information. Do not attach a copy of the original FBAR. An amendment should not be made until at least **120** calendar days after the original FBAR is filed.

Record Keeping Requirements. Persons required to file an FBAR must retain records that contain the name in which each account is maintained, the number or other designation of the account, the name and address of the foreign financial institution that maintains the account, the type of account, and the maximum account value of each account during the reporting period. The records must be retained for a period of 5 years from June 30th of the year following the calendar year reported and must be available for inspection as provided by law. Retaining a copy of the filed FBAR can help to satisfy the record keeping requirements.

An officer or employee who files an FBAR to report signature authority over an employer's foreign financial account is not required to personally retain records regarding these accounts.

Questions. FBAR help is available by telephone or e-mail. Call 866-270-0733 (toll-free within the U.S.) or 313-234-6146 (from outside the U.S., not toll-free) from 8 a.m.—4:30 p.m. Eastern time, or e-mail your inquiry to FBARquestions@irs.gov.

Explanations for Specific Items

Part I — Filer Information

Item 1. The FBAR is an annual report. Enter the calendar year being reported. If amending a previously filed FBAR, check the "Amended" box.

Item 2. Check the box that describes the filer. Check only one box. Individuals reporting only signature authority, check box "a". If filing a consolidated FBAR, check box "d". To determine if a consolidated FBAR can be filed, see Part V. If the type of filer is not listed in boxes "a" through "c", check box "e", and enter the type of filer. Persons that should check box "e" include, but are not limited to, trusts, estates, limited liability companies, and tax-exempt entities (even if the entity is organized as a corporation). A disregarded entity must check box "e", and enter the type of entity followed by "(D.E.)". For example, a limited liability company that is disregarded for United States federal tax purposes would enter "limited liability company (D.E.)".

Item 3. Provide the filer's United States taxpayer identification number. Generally, this is the filer's United States social security number (SSN), United States individual taxpayer identification number (ITIN), or employer identification number (EIN). Throughout the FBAR, numbers should be entered with no spaces, dashes, or other punctuation. If the filer does NOT have a United States taxpayer identification number, complete Item 4.

Item 4. Complete Item 4 only if the filer does NOT have a United States taxpayer identification number. Item 4 requires the filer to provide information from an official foreign government document to verify the filer's nationality or residence. Enter the document number followed by the country of issuance, check the appropriate type of document, and if "other" is checked, provide the type of document.

Item 5. If the filer is an individual, enter the filer's date of birth, using the month, day, and year convention.

Items 9, 10, 11, 12, and 13. Enter the filer's address. An individual residing in the United States must enter the street address of the individual's United States residence, not a post office box. An individual residing outside the United States must enter the individual's United States mailing address. If the individual does not have a United States mailing address, the individual must enter a foreign residence address. An entity must enter its United States mailing address. If the entity does not have a United States mailing address, the entity must enter its foreign mailing address.

Item 14. If the filer has a financial interest in 25 or more foreign financial accounts, check "Yes" and enter the number of accounts. Do not complete Part II or Part III of the FBAR. If filing a consolidated FBAR, only complete Part V, Items 34-42, for each United States entity included in the consolidated FBAR.

Note. If the filer has signature authority over 25 or more foreign financial accounts, only complete Part IV, Items 34-43, for each person for which the filer has signature authority, and check "No" in Part I, Item 14.

Filers must comply with applicable recording keeping requirements. See Record Keeping Requirements.

Part II — Information on Financial Account(s) Owned Separately

Enter information in the applicable parts of the form only. Number the pages used, and mail only those pages. If there is not enough space to provide all account information, copy and complete additional pages of the required Part as necessary. Do not use any attachments unless otherwise specified in the instructions.

Item 15. Determining Maximum Account Value.

Step 1. Determine the maximum value of each account (in the currency of that account) during the calendar year being reported. The maximum value of an account is a reasonable approximation of the greatest value of currency or nonmonetary assets in the account during the calendar year. Periodic account statements may be relied on to determine the maximum value of the account, provided that the statements fairly reflect the maximum account value during the calendar year. For Item 15, if the filer had a financial interest in more than one account, each account must be valued separately.

Step 2. In the case of non-United States currency, convert the maximum account value for each account into United States dollars. Convert foreign currency by using the Treasury's Financial Management Service rate (this rate may be found at www.fms.treas.gov) from the last day of the calendar year. If no Treasury Financial Management Service rate is available, use another verifiable exchange rate and provide the source of that rate. In valuing currency of a country that uses multiple exchange rates, use the rate that would apply if the currency in the account were converted into United States dollars on the last day of the calendar year.

If the aggregate of the maximum account values exceeds $10,000, an FBAR must be filed. An FBAR is not required to be filed if the person did not have $10,000 of aggregate value in foreign financial accounts at any time during the calendar year.

For United States persons with a financial interest in or signature authority over fewer than 25 accounts that are unable to determine if the aggregate maximum account values of the accounts exceeded $10,000 at any time during the calendar year, complete Part II, III, IV, or V, as appropriate, for each of these accounts and enter "value unknown" in Item 15.

Item 16. Indicate the type of account. Check only one box. If "Other" is selected, describe the account.

Item 17. Provide the name of the financial institution with which the account is held.

Item 18. Provide the account number that the financial institution uses to designate the account.

Items 19-23. Provide the complete mailing address of the financial institution where the account is located. If the foreign address does not include a state (e.g., province) or postal code, leave the box(es) blank.

Part III — Information on Financial Account(s) Owned Jointly

Enter information in the applicable parts of the form only. Number the pages used, and mail only those pages. If there is not enough space to provide all account information, copy and complete additional pages of the required Part as necessary. Do not use any attachments unless otherwise specified in the instructions.

For Items 15-23, see Part II. Each joint owner must report the entire value of the account as determined under Item 15.

Item 24. Enter the number of joint owners for the account. If the exact number is not known, provide an estimate. Do not count the filer when determining the number of joint owners.

Items 25-33. Use the identifying information of the principal joint owner (excluding the filer) to complete Items 25-33. Leave blank items for which no information is available. If the filer's spouse has an interest in a jointly owned account, the filer's spouse is the principal joint owner. Enter "(spouse)" on line 26 after the last name of the joint spousal owner. See Exceptions, Certain Accounts Jointly Owned by Spouses, to determine if the filer's spouse is required to independently report the jointly owned accounts.

Part IV — Information on Financial Account(s) Where Filer has Signature Authority but No Financial Interest in the Account(s)

Enter information in the applicable parts of the form only. Number the pages used, and mail only those pages. If there is not enough space to provide all account information, copy and complete additional pages of the required Part as necessary. Do not use any attachments unless otherwise specified in the instructions.

25 or More Foreign Financial Accounts. Filers with signature authority over 25 or more foreign financial accounts must complete only Items 34-43 for each person on whose behalf the filer has signature authority.

Modified Reporting for United States Persons Residing and Employed Outside of the United States. A United States person who **(1)** resides outside of the United States, **(2)** is an officer or employee of an employer who is physically located outside of the United States, and **(3)** has signature authority over a foreign financial account that is owned or maintained by the individual's employer should only complete Part I and Part IV, Items 34-43 of the FBAR. Part IV, Items 34-43 should only be completed one time with information about the individual's employer.

For Items 15-23, see Part II.

Items 34-42. Provide the name, address, and identifying number of the owner of the foreign financial account for which the individual has signature authority over but no financial interest in the account. If there is more than one owner of the account for which the individual has signature authority, provide the information in Items 34-42 for the principal joint owner (excluding the filer). If account information is completed for more than one account of the same owner, identify the owner only once and write "Same Owner" in Item 34 for the succeeding accounts with the same owner.

Item 43. Enter filer's title for the position that provides signature authority (e.g., treasurer).

Part V — Information on Financial Account(s) Where Filer Is Filing a Consolidated Report

Enter information in the applicable parts of the form only. Number the pages used, and mail only those pages. If there is not enough space to provide all account information, copy and complete additional pages of the required Part as necessary. Do not use any attachments unless otherwise specified in the instructions.

Who Can File a Consolidated FBAR. An entity that is a United States person that owns directly or indirectly a greater than 50 percent interest in another entity that is required to file an FBAR is permitted to file a consolidated FBAR on behalf of itself and such other entity. Check box "d" in Part I, Item 2 and complete Part V. If filing a consolidated FBAR and reporting 25 or more foreign financial accounts, complete only Items 34-42 for each entity included in the consolidated FBAR.

For Items 15-23, see Part II.

Items 34-42. Provide the name, United States taxpayer identification number, and address of the owner of the foreign financial account as shown on the books of the financial institution. If account information is completed for more than one account of the same owner, identify the owner only once and write "Same Owner" in Item 34 for the succeeding accounts of the same owner.

Signatures

Items 44-46. The FBAR must be signed by the filer named in Part I. If the FBAR is being filed on behalf of a partnership, corporation, limited liability company, trust, estate, or other entity, it must be signed by an authorized individual. Enter the authorized individual's title in Item 45.

An individual must leave "Filer's Title" blank, unless the individual is filing an FBAR due to the individual's signature authority. If an individual is filing because the individual has signature authority over a foreign financial account, the individual should enter the title upon which his or her authority is based in Item 45.

A spouse included as a joint owner, who does not file a separate FBAR in accordance with the instructions in Part III, must also sign the FBAR (in Item 44) for the jointly owned accounts. See the instructions for Part III.

Penalties

A person who is required to file an FBAR and fails to properly file may be subject to a civil penalty not to exceed $10,000 per violation. If there is reasonable cause for the failure and the balance in the account is properly reported, no penalty will be imposed. A person who willfully fails to report an account or account identifying information may be subject to a civil monetary penalty equal to the greater of $100,000 or 50 percent of the balance in the account at the time of the violation. See 31 U.S.C. section 5321(a)(5). Willful violations may also be subject to criminal penalties under 31 U.S.C. section 5322(a), 31 U.S.C. section 5322(b), or 18 U.S.C. section 1001.

Index

www.ingramcontent.com/pod-product-compliance
Lightning Source LLC
Chambersburg PA
CBHW081217170526
45165CB00009B/2853